Granny's

Book of
Good Old-Fashioned

Common Sense

Granny's
Book of
Good Old-Fashioned
Common Sense

Linda Gray

BLACK & WHITE PUBLISHING

First published 2007
by Black & White Publishing Ltd
99 Giles Street, Edinburgh EH6 6BZ

1 3 5 7 9 10 8 6 4 2 07 08 09 10 11

ISBN 13: 978 1 84502 180 1
ISBN 10: 1 84502 180 0

A CIP catalogue record for this book is available from the British Library.

Typeset by Ellipsis Books Limited, Glasgow
Printed by MPG Books Ltd, Bodmin, Cornwall

Contents

COMMON SENSE

Common sense: noun or adjective - good and sound judgment in practical matters. From the Latin *sensus communis*. Can be interpreted as an opinion of what most people's experience would consider to be the prudent and appropriate course of action to be taken, based upon knowledge that is common to most people.

Common sense features in many popular sayings such as 'He does not have the **common sense** he was born with', '**Common sense** is not so common' and 'Fortunately, she had the **common sense** to get as far away as possible'.

Common sense also features in classic literature:

'The records in our newspapers, the late exposure by *The Lancet*, and the **common sense** and senses of common people, furnish too abundant evidence against both defences'.

Our Mutual Friend by Charles Dickens

'To impute such a design to Lady Susan would be taking from her every claim to that excellent understanding which her bitterest enemies have never denied her; and equally low must sink my pretensions to **common sense** if I am suspected of matrimonial views in my behaviour to her'

Lady Susan by Jane Austen

For Laura, Shay, Jodie and Lucy . . . I wouldn't have done it without you!

Introduction

Stay-at-home mums of the past never had a moment to spare with all the household chores that had to be done by hand. Nowadays, mums have precious few moments to spare simply because the pace of life is always one step ahead. However, what we do have nowadays is power: power to make our own decisions; power to take on the world; and without, if we choose, the obligatory band of gold of yesteryear. And we have power too in the form of energy – electricity to run all our time-saving gadgets.

If our grandmothers had had electricity, what would they have done with all that extra time? If we didn't have TV, what would we do with all that extra time? Twenty minutes here, a forty-five-minute documentary there – and what about all the soaps? Gulp . . . time management is, in the great scheme of things, a simple case of priorities.

If you're yearning for a change of lifestyle but honestly don't know what to do if the TV's not on, check out the ideas on the following pages for a slice of life from days gone past and brought straight into the present. Turn off the TV (it'll be painless – really!) and browse through the wonderful selection of old-fashioned recipes and crafts re-designed for today's tastes.

Join Granny in the kitchen and try out lots of basic recipes with a 'today' taste. With a fridge in the kitchen you can produce designer leftovers, saving time and washing-up. Turn out a traditional shepherd's pie or a pot of strawberry jam for lots of brownie points!

Join Granny in the garden and learn how to make the most of your garden space. Treat your family to fresh organic fruit and veg. Cook nourishing meals with home produce. By following a few simple ideas you can reduce the workload and increase your crops.

Join Granny in the parlour and make beautiful creations for your home and family. From fun stuff for the kids to elegant knitwear and stunning embroidery – all from a length of yarn and a needle or two. And you don't need a degree in rocket science!

Join Granny in the nursery and spend quality time with the children. No plugs or batteries needed, just a few simple tools will bring laughter and enjoyment to everyone in the family aged from five to ninety-five. And before bed, read a traditional fairy story to encourage magical dreams!

Step into the natural world of yesterday with all the knowledge and information of today.

Enjoy your own organic fruit and vegetables, home-made clothes and toys and good old-fashioned parlour games for a brighter future for you and your family for generations to come.

Part One

In the Kitchen

Household Tips and Tricks

Without the equipment and gadgets we have at our disposal today, housewives of yesteryear would have been obliged to do a lot more actual 'housework' than we do now. However, let's not assume they were gluttons for punishment! They had all sorts of tricks and useful ideas to cut their workload, some of which we could use today.

General Cleaning

Cutting the Cleaning Bill
Our homes are full of products. Bathroom cleaners, kitchen cleaners, oven cleaners, washing powders and conditioners, washing-up liquids and dishwasher products, toilet rolls, shampoos and so on. Cut a big chunk out of your shopping bill – don't buy them!

You may have to buy the conditioner and style shampoo for the fifteen-year-old in the house or risk a moody but many other products can be replaced with alternatives. Try these to get you started.

Does your kitchen cleaner have added lemon? Well, forget the rest – the lemon is all you need! Save the ends of lemons and rub over ceramic surfaces. Rinse with clean water. The natural bleaching agent in lemons magically lifts most stains clean away!

Cut down on washing-up detergents. If the dishes have had no contact with grease, they only need a rinse with clean warm water. And they won't need drying up either. Just leave them to dry naturally.

Invest in a decent polishing cloth. You can make your furniture shine without piling on commercial polish every time you dust. Find a soft non-abrasive cloth that doesn't fluff up when you use it.

Instead of buying tumble-drier products to get that 'just hung out' aroma, try it for real – time and space permitting. The laundry will smell fresher and you'll also save on the electricity the tumble-drier isn't using!

Look for user-friendly products. Liquid detergents are often better for your washing machine than powders – they don't clog up the works so quickly, avoiding the plumber's bill.

As for toilet rolls, well, unless you happen to live in a nice private forest with lots of fig trees available, the alternatives are limited!

Cut down on the cleaning products and your health, your environment and your pocket will be a lot better off!

Cleaning Saucepans and Baking Dishes
Don't stand at the sink for ages moaning about the washing-up. You know the dishwasher won't remove the hard stuck-on food either. The best thing to do is put it off till tomorrow! Soak the dishes or saucepan in water with a drop of washing-up liquid or lemon juice and leave overnight. OK, the kitchen doesn't look pristine, but time management counts in a busy household!

Cleaning Rugs
Find an old tennis racket or something similar; make sure you can grip it firmly by the handle with two hands. Hang the rug over the washing line, cover your mouth and nose with a builder's mask or a scarf and beat the rug for all you're worth. It's great for getting rid of a bad mood as well as getting your rugs all clean and fresh. A perfect remedy for PMT!

Clean Beds

We lose moisture during the night which takes about twenty minutes or more to evaporate when we leave our beds in the morning. Throw back the covers and let the bed dry out for half an hour before making it. If you leave the house even sooner after waking (!) simply smooth the sheet, plump up the pillows and leave the quilt turned back for the day. The bed will keep a lot fresher and sweeter smelling, which means you may not have to wash the sheets so often!

Laundry Tricks

Keep the washing until you have full loads, rather than doing it as and when it turns up in the washing basket. It may feel like you are keeping on top of it, but it is all too tempting to throw a mixed load in and then land up with everything light pink or a dirty grey colour!

Shake all items out and empty pockets to make the most of the wash. When you tightly pack clothes, they don't wash as well. And paraphernalia in the pockets can seriously damage the health of your washing machine.

The Airing Cupboard

Keep the airing cupboard tidy and everyone in the house will be able to find their own bedding and towels etc. Fold up a whole set of bedding together. A sheet, quilt cover and pillow cases neatly stacked in one pile makes it so much quicker and easier to find everything when making all the beds. And it also stops the possibility of everything getting pulled out and made untidy while searching for a matching pillowcase.

Fold the towels 'health club' style for a professional look! Fold in half lengthwise and then tuck the ends into the middle.

Ninety Per Cent Less Ironing

Ironing or pressing cloth reduces its lifespan considerably. Pressing may give an outwardly smooth appearance but under the surface lies a tangled mess of overworked fibres. If you absolutely hate ironing or simply want to get rid of a pressing chore, there is a solution!

As soon as the washing machine has finished the final spin, take your wash load and hang it on a washing line, preferably outside, weather permitting.

Shake each item before pegging it out, and pull jeans into shape. This takes only a few seconds. When the washing is dry, or as dry as it's going to get today, bring it indoors.

Air the wash load by folding carefully and putting in an airing or warming cupboard until finished or, if the heating is on, hang over radiators. Make sure the items are smooth and not 'bunched up' anywhere or you will double your ironing chore!

If there's a delay in hanging your washing, take it out of the washing machine and fold it all carefully, smoothing and gently pulling each item into shape. Then hang up as soon as you can. Smoothing and folding damp washing eliminates lots of unnecessary creases, and everything that doesn't get a fibre-crushing treatment will live a whole lot longer and it takes only seconds to smooth and fold.

Now, the moment of truth! Go through your dry, clean washing and only iron what *needs* to be ironed! Towels, sheets, jumpers, underwear and (home) working clothes should never need ironing. Be bold and fold your towels neatly away, and enjoy the freedom of a much smaller task to get through. Towels will seem much thicker and 'bouncier' if they haven't been ironed.

Make a mental note of the material used for clothes you know you need never iron. When you go shopping for clothes next time, remember that mental note and choose carefully.

Stains and Discoloured Cloth

Whites that aren't quite white any more will get a new lease of life if soaked in a bowl of water with cream of tartar added. Allow 1 teaspoon of cream of tartar to 2 pints of water.

Before washing clothes with old stains on them, try rubbing a little glycerine into the mark to soften it before treating with stain remover or regular detergent. Some modern fabrics won't respond to these treatments but many will so give it a go. It's worth trying to eliminate that greyish tint to whites.

Coffee

An old-fashioned way of removing coffee stains is to mix the yolk of an egg with a little warm water and use it like soap. Rub into the stained part and then rinse with tepid water.

Blood

Spread a little starch on to the stained part and leave for a few hours. Then wash the item as usual.

Cocoa

Chocolate and cocoa spills should be sponged straight away with cold water. Don't use hot water. Then wash the item as you would normally.

Wine

Wine spilled on a linen or cotton tablecloth can be difficult to remove. If the stain is old, soften with a little glycerine first. Otherwise put the stained part in boiling milk. Then wash with soap and water. If that doesn't work, try applying some salt and add a few drops of lemon juice and leave for an hour or two before washing.

Cooking Tips

Don't you just cringe when some clever kitchen-type person tells you what you could be doing with the leftovers in the fridge, when it's plainly obvious the leftovers will stay there until they walk out by themselves!

Leftover meals of old used to be the norm. Housewives were at home all day every day and knew the insides of their pantries better than we could possibly ever know the inside of our fridge/freezers! More often than not, saving money with leftovers, although a great idea, takes a lot of time in preparation and relies on many other ingredients being available. So . . .

Design your own Leftovers!

Cooking twice as much as you need 'by design' allows you the extra time tomorrow with the added bonus of knowing what you're going to cook.

Dithering around in the kitchen working out who wants what and what you forgot to buy, takes ages. If you know you've already got a portion of the evening meal ready in the fridge, life becomes a lot less stressful.

One-Pot Meals

Most 'in-the-pot' dishes like bolognaise, chilli, casseroles and stews can all be made in double quantities in very little extra time. Make sure you thoroughly reheat meat dishes until piping hot. The only real problem with in-the-pot recipes is that you're obliged to eat the same meal two nights in a row. To get around this, make a bolognaise one night served with pasta and add a spicy chilli sauce to the leftovers for the following evening's meal and serve with rice or potatoes.

Basic Bolognaise

Thoroughly cook minced beef – or vegetarian equivalent – and set aside. Gently fry, in a little oil, a chopped onion and green pepper. Then add sliced mushrooms and stir gently over a low heat until the mushrooms are just beginning to cook. Add the minced beef, stir and mix together thoroughly.

Pour in a tin of chopped tomatoes with the juice – or use fresh tomatoes if available. Add a little tomato purée to thicken the sauce and, if liked, add a tin of drained red kidney beans. Cook mixture over a low heat until thoroughly hot right through. Stir in a little chopped fresh basil just before the end of cooking time if you have some. Serve with cooked spaghetti or any other kind of pasta. Sprinkle over a little Parmesan or grated cheese to bring out the tomato taste.

Chilli

Make a bolognaise dish, cool and cover. Refrigerate overnight. Stir in some chilli spices and heat the whole dish thoroughly until piping hot – NB: always make sure re-heated food is piping hot right through. Serve chilli with cooked rice (make too much so you can use leftover rice the next day – carry on reading for rice ideas), or with jacket potatoes or a green salad. Jacket potatoes can also be used in a leftover dish.

Casseroles and Stews

Make a basic stew by gently browning cubed beef steak – or vegetarian equivalent – in a large heavy-based saucepan with a little oil. Make a stock to add to the meat – either a gravy using instant gravy powder or make your own from a brown meat stock. Add to the saucepan with a tin of chopped tomatoes (or 3 or 4 fresh chopped tomatoes if available). Then stir in whatever vegetables you like. Sliced carrots are always a favourite in stews and go particularly well with beef. Chop some onions, leeks, swede, turnips or parsnips – whatever you have that the family likes to eat.

The stew pot can cover just about anything you want! Add some pearl barley for a healthy eating addition – and bulk. Potatoes can also be added of course – although it's best to leave them until the last half hour of cooking time or they tend to go mushy.

Simmer the stew for a couple of hours if possible – or at least until all the vegetables are tender. Serve steaming hot on its own in a large bowl, or pick out the meat and vegetables and serve with roast potatoes then use the stock as gravy.

Bay leaves or a bouquet garni (see p. 21) add flavour to stews. Remove before serving.

Stews are perfect eaten the next day. Leave to cool, refrigerate then heat through until piping hot. After marinating overnight in their own juices, the meat and vegetables are especially delicious!

Rice

I always manage to cook enough rice to feed the neighbourhood so I have had to learn what to do with the leftovers!

Let the rice cool completely, place in a bowl, cover with plastic food wrap, and refrigerate. It's very important the rice is refrigerated as soon as it's cool. The following evening you have a base for a new and exciting meal.

NB: never use rice that has been left out of the fridge overnight, especially in the warm weather, as it begins to ferment and can make you ill.

Egg Fried Rice
Make a plain one- or two-egg omelette and remove from pan. (A drop or two of soy sauce can be added to the egg mixture if liked.) Cut into small pieces and set aside. Put cold leftover rice in the pan with a little sunflower, nut or olive oil and stir gently. Add omelette pieces, stir and heat until hot right through. Serve with Chinese-style ribs or veggie sausages.

Special Fried Rice
Fry, in a little olive or nut oil, a finely chopped onion, tomato, green pepper and a few sliced mushrooms. Add cold, cooked rice to pan. Stir gently and cook

through until rice is piping hot. Add sweetcorn and a few chopped walnuts if liked. Serve with any meat, fish, egg or veggie dish. Or enjoy on its own.

Rice Salad

In a large bowl, mix leftover cold cooked rice with fresh raw chopped vegetables; onion, tomato, sweet pepper, celery, sweetcorn, and any other favourites hanging around in the fridge. Chill for half an hour before serving. A half mayo, half natural yoghurt dressing can be gently stirred in if liked, or serve separately: mix equal portions of mayonnaise and natural yoghurt with a few chopped chives or other preferred herbs.

Cold Rice Complete Meal

To create a whole summer meal in a bowl, mix cold rice with chopped boiled egg, cooked flaked fish, pieces of ham or cooked chicken. Add finely chopped salad vegetables and a few nuts and sunflower seeds if you have them. For a veggie alternative, try cold cooked veggie sausages, sliced, or tofu mixed with the rice.

Potatoes

Potatoes can easily be turned into 'designer leftovers'.

Jackets

Cooking a whole tray of jacket potatoes will take no longer than cooking one or two – just a few extra minutes scrubbing time is needed. Store leftovers in the fridge, then choose one of the following ideas to feed the family the following evening.

Flat Fries

Slice and shallow-fry leftover jackets in hot olive oil and some mixed dried herbs or cumin spice. Turn occasionally. Serve hot with anything. Use as little oil as possible as fried food tends to be high in calories and saturated fats.

Family Omelette

Peel and dice leftover jackets and gently fry in olive oil, with a chopped onion. Pour over beaten eggs and add some grated cheese. Other vegetables can be added to the omelette such as cooked peas or chopped onion, or both. Cook gently for a few minutes. Turn and cook the other side. The omelette will probably fall apart during this manoeuvre. Just push it back together. No one will know! Serve hot with a green salad.

Rough Potato Salad

Peel leftover jackets and chop roughly. Mix in a large bowl with sweetcorn, tuna and a little chopped onion or chives. Delicious with a mayonnaise sauce or natural yoghurt, stirred gently into the potato mix or served separately.

Mashed Potato

Hot mashed potato, served with a delicious gravy, is always a family favourite. Make twice as much and delight the family two days in a row! Cool the leftover mash thoroughly. Place in a bowl, cover with plastic food wrap and refrigerate.

Baked Mash

Put leftover mash into a large bowl and stir in cooked, flaked, white fish, cooked bacon pieces, or cooked vegetables. Place in a greased ovenproof dish, top with grated cheese and bake in a medium oven until piping hot right through. Serve with hot tomatoes or a salad.

Burger Mash

In a large bowl, mix leftover mash with a little beaten egg, some chopped chives or very finely chopped onion. Then form small balls of the mixture in your hands. Flatten slightly and, if available, coat with breadcrumbs or chopped nuts. Fry gently on both sides in a little hot olive or nut oil. Drain on kitchen paper and serve with green vegetables or salad.

Cottage Pie

Cook some minced beef, or a veggie equivalent, a chopped onion and a tin of tomatoes together and place mixture in a large lightly greased ovenproof dish. Spoon leftover mashed potato over the top, and sprinkle on a little grated cheese, if liked. Heat through thoroughly in a medium to hot oven and serve hot with green vegetables.

Bubble and Squeak

This is a very traditional English dish that Granny would have made regularly. Put leftover mashed potato with cooked and chopped spring greens or cabbage in a bowl and mix together thoroughly. Form into small flat cakes or simply fill the pan and make one large piece to cut later. Fry in a little hot oil until thoroughly heated right through. Serve with sausages or gammon steaks.

Chicken

Cook a slightly larger chicken and keep the leftovers covered – and maybe hidden – in the fridge. A vegetarian equivalent of chicken will work equally well with these dishes.

Quick Chicken Curry

Pour a home-made curry sauce or a jar of ready-made sauce over cut-up leftover chicken pieces and heat thoroughly in a hot oven. Always make sure re-heated meat is piping hot right through before consuming. Serve with rice or jacket potatoes.

Chicken Salad

Mix cold leftover chicken with a finely chopped onion and stir in a half mayo, half natural yoghurt dressing. Add a few walnuts for an extra special treat. Chill for 30 minutes and serve with any dish or on its own.

Chicken Stir Fry

Put cut-up chicken pieces in a frying pan with a little olive or nut oil. Mix in thinly sliced sweet peppers, onion, tomato and any other bits in the fridge that look healthy enough to eat. Cook gently for a few minutes, ensuring the chicken is thoroughly hot. Then mix into a bowl of hot cooked noodles. Serve with an oriental style sauce.

Chicken Rice

Cut cooked chicken into small pieces and mix with cold rice, chopped green and red peppers and a tablespoon or two of sweet corn kernels. Serve as a main course with a green salad. If you have a few unsalted nuts of any kind, mix them into the chicken or the salad.

Final Hot Tip

Roughly planning a few menus in advance will mean you are always in control of nourishing and tasty meals and have no need to lean guiltily on the microwave waiting for the latest TV dinner to cook!

Fresh Food

How Available Was It?

Although in the past there weren't microwave meals and takeaways, one very healthy eating habit that has taken a back seat through the decades and one which we are all endeavouring to re-establish is *fresh food*. There is nothing so nourishing as fresh fruit and veg.

The five-a-day rule should be something we all stick to for a healthy body, mind and spirit!

Back in the 1950s in the UK, ration books were still being phased out after the war years and there were fewer varieties of fruit and vegetables available in the high street – pre-supermarket years, the old-fashioned greengrocer and the market stall were the only places to buy our produce unless we grew it ourselves.

Root crops and greens were nearly always available, although during some parts of the year, the crops that had been stored for a few months were not in the condition we would expect today. Potatoes were just potatoes at the beginning of autumn – then as winter progressed they were called 'old' potatoes, followed by the 'new' potatoes in the shops in spring and early summer. And the old potatoes really were old!

Root vegetables are eaten more in moderate and cool climates and they certainly work well in casseroles, soups and stews. In the 1950s, the most available roots would have been potatoes, carrots, turnip and swede.

Peas and runner beans, marrow and salad ingredients were on sale according to their growing season. There were few vegetables and fruits imported, although bananas and oranges were available, as were peaches and grapes. However, these more exotic foods tended to be rather expensive for the average housewife to buy regularly.

Peas and runner beans were very popular – probably more so because of the seasonal quality. If you can only get something at a certain time of the year, you appreciate it so much more! Marrows were also grown – surprisingly we didn't tend to eat the baby marrows as courgettes like we do nowadays.

Green veg was available most of the year because we can grow spring greens and cabbage through more than one season in the UK.

Onions were nearly always available in some form. In late spring and early summer, when the stored onions were too soft to eat or had started sprouting again, spring onions were very popular.

How did we cope without tinned tomatoes? They just didn't exist in the UK in those early years. If you needed to make a tomato sauce you would have had to go to the market at the end of the day and buy up all the mushy fresh tomatoes at a low price – then make your own!

Through the following two decades, the '60s and '70s, many more vegetables and fruits were imported and more varieties were grown under glass in this country.

Mushrooms became a family favourite and everybody learned to stop believing that all mushrooms must be toadstools if grown outside of a sterile environment!

Peppers, sweet and chilli, were becoming more used in everyday family meals, and with the introduction of tinned tomatoes, the sky was the limit!

Unfortunately, during the high-powered racy world of the '80s and '90s, fast food in the shape of takeaways and microwavable TV dinners became so popular that many of us never got around to learning basic cooking skills. Inevitably we have denied ourselves one of the most basic pleasures, in the form of a home-cooked family meal.

Saturated fats were used more in the '50s and '60s but because most of us had a more demanding physical life – washing by hand etc. – and few gadgets to reduce the workload, the fats tended to work themselves off a lot easier. Rather than dump the washing machine – heaven forbid! – we can adjust the recipes for today's way of life simply by reducing the saturated fat content. Everything else works just fine!

Family Meals

One of the most enjoyable things about pre-TV years was the fact that families tended to sit down around a table to eat together, mulling over the day's events and generally coming together. It's a habit worth reviving if you have a dining table and can gather all the members of the family together at one time! Here are a few recipes that would have been served in those days gone by.

Breakfasts

Boiled Egg and Soldiers!

The saying 'she couldn't even boil an egg' used to be applied to someone who couldn't cook. Well, nowadays there are plenty of us who have never had a boiled egg – in the traditional egg cup – and probably don't even know what a 'soldier' is! So it's very likely that there are a number of us who don't know how to boil an egg.

However, it's as easy as falling off a wall!

Ingredients and Equipment

eggs – allow 1–2 per person
bread – allow 1–2 slices per person
butter (or equivalent)
a small saucepan
an eggcup and a spoon
a small plate

Method

Put eggs into a small saucepan and cover with water. Place on the heat and bring water to the boil. Meanwhile, prepare a plate with an eggcup and teaspoon and make the soldiers!

Butter one side of the bread, cut in half then cut into finger slices. Arrange on the plate.

When the water is boiling, use an old-fashioned egg timer or a regular everyday clock to time the eggs. For a very soft-boiled egg, allow 3 minutes of boiling time. Boiling an egg for 10 minutes will give you a solid hard-boiled egg suitable for sandwiches or mixed into salad dishes.

Normally an egg will be boiled for anything between 3 and 7 minutes if eaten on its own. To make what children often call a 'dippy' egg, don't boil for longer than 4 to 5 minutes depending on the size of egg. If the yolk is soft then the 'soldiers' can be dipped into the yolk.

When the time is up, remove the egg from the water using a large slotted spoon to drain the water. Carefully tip the egg, narrow side up, into the eggcup. Either peel the shell from the top part of the egg or, using a sharp knife, cut the top off. The shell will be very hot so care is needed when peeling. (See p. 73 for how to put your eggshells to good use.)

Enjoy while still hot.

The Famous British Fry-Up

The British have a reputation, especially throughout Europe, for eating a very unhealthy fry-up for breakfast every morning. Apart from builders stopping for a much-needed breakfast in a local greasy cafe, I can't imagine anyone subjecting their bodies to that sort of treatment every day of the week. Maybe on a Sunday as a special 'treat'.

The worst part of a fry-up is of course the 'fry' word. Whereas our parents and grandparents may have fried in good old-fashioned dripping, we just don't do that any more – thank goodness!

To enjoy the best of the ingredients in a fried breakfast, avoid frying as much as possible. Bacon, sausages and tomatoes can all be grilled. Choose lean bacon and maybe even veggie sausages – or a home-made variety from your local butcher. Eggs can be boiled or scrambled. Mushrooms can be sliced and gently simmered in a little water. And fried bread can be substituted with toast and a light spread.

Ingredients
    (per person)
    1–2 rashers of lean bacon
    1–2 sausages
    a few mushrooms, sliced
    1 tomato
    1–2 eggs
    1–2 slices of bread

Method

The sausages will take the longest time to cook so start them off under a moderate grill. Prick them a few times with a fork to allow the fat to drain out. Prepare all other ingredients and put the plates in a warm place. Put the water on to boil if you are boiling eggs.

If you are scrambling your eggs, beat the eggs into a bowl and add a little milk. To spice the eggs up a little, mix in a teaspoon of prepared mustard or maybe a little grated cheese.

Slice mushrooms and halve tomatoes. Put a small pan of water on the heat for the mushrooms.

When the sausages are at least half cooked, put the eggs on to boil or, if scrambling, add to a pan with a knob of butter or low fat equivalent. Put the bacon and tomatoes under the grill and add the mushrooms to a pan of boiling water. Keep scrambled eggs on a low heat and stir regularly with a wooden spoon.

Turn over the bacon and tomatoes during cooking time. When everything is cooked, put the toast into the toaster and start dishing up the food on to warm plates. Butter the toast and enjoy while still piping hot.

Kedgeree

Kedgeree derives from an Indian dish called *khichri*. The well-to-do in India, and in Britain, during Victorian times of lavish meals, were served breakfast of a fish and rice dish often spiced with seasonal herbs. Fish was thought to be best served in the morning. During the hot summer months, it would have gone bad by the evening, with no fridges or cold spots available to store it.

Kedgeree is eaten more as a light dinner or lunch nowadays but is still a perfectly acceptable and indeed very nourishing breakfast meal. If you are trying to lose weight, a healthy full breakfast is an especially good start to the day.

Ingredients

smoked haddock
boiled or steamed basmati or long grain white rice
hard-boiled eggs (allow 1 per person)
curry powder or sauce if liked or any seasonal herbs
finely chopped spring onions or shallots
cooking oil or butter
a sprig of parsley to garnish

Method

Poach the fish in a pan of boiling water or steam if preferred. Cool and flake, making sure all bones are removed.

Shell the hard-boiled eggs and chop finely. Make sure all shell is removed.

Mix the fish and eggs into the cooked rice and stir gently. Add curry powder, sauce or other herbs and chopped onions and thoroughly mix all ingredients.

Put the mixture into a large pan or wok and stir gently over a low heat until piping hot right through. Serve immediately, garnished with parsley.

For a rich and very high-calorie meal, stir in 3 or 4 tablespoons of cream!

Kedgeree is a versatile recipe and can be adapted according to seasonal vegetables and whatever happens to be in the cupboard. Try different types of fish or add some garlic to the dish. Fresh coriander leaves are a tasty alternative to curry powder and a curry paste could also be used, although the paste must be mixed thoroughly before serving.

Oatmeal (or porridge oats)

Traditionally known as a Scottish breakfast, porridge oats have long been a hearty and nourishing breakfast meal. For generations past, oats have been known to be extremely good for you and in recent years, scientists have proved the point. There are so many qualities in the humble bowl of porridge, they can hardly be listed but here goes:

- The constituents in oats help soothe the nervous system and so can reduce nicotine cravings.
- A bowl of porridge in the morning will keep you feeling fuller for longer – so reducing the need to snack.
- Oats contain a chemical which helps break down fatty deposits and so reduce the risk of heart disease.
- Porridge is high in vitamin B6, which helps the brain produce serotonin – so makes you feel good.
- And it can even sort out hormonal balances – improving your sex life!

So it would seem a bowl of porridge in the morning is just about the best way to start the day. Stop smoking, lose weight, feel good and be healthy – all from a cereal bowl!

Ingredients

    rolled oats
    water or milk or a mixture of both
    a little sugar or honey – optional

Method

Place the oats in a heavy-bottomed pan and add milk or water – or both (1 cup of oats to 2–3 cups of fluid is the usual proportion). If you prefer your porridge to be thicker, use less fluid; for a runnier porridge, use more.

Mix well and stir over a low heat until the milk has been absorbed by the oats. Cook for a further minute or two until the oats are soft.

Pour or spoon into a bowl and sprinkle on a little sugar or spoon over a teaspoon or two of honey if liked. Eat while hot.

Soups

Tomato Soup

There are many variations on a regular home-made tomato soup. And don't be fooled into thinking that you shouldn't bother because there are any number available in cans and packets in every shop you go in. There is nothing tastier than a home-made tomato soup, especially if you have grown the tomatoes yourself as well. But even if they are bought tomatoes, making a tomato soup really isn't hard and will be a delight to all the family. The following recipe is a basic summer tomato soup hearty enough to serve on its own or with a warm crusty loaf. This recipe will serve 4 or more people depending on the size of your saucepan and the quantity of tomatoes used!

Ingredients

    1 small potato, peeled and diced
    1 small onion, peeled and chopped
    a little butter or cooking oil
    chicken or vegetable stock
    as many tomatoes as the pan will hold
    chopped fresh basil if available or any seasonal herbs

Method

In a large saucepan, gently cook the diced potato and chopped onion in the butter or cooking oil. Stir until softened and be very careful not to burn the butter or vegetables. Remove from the heat. Peel all the tomatoes and chop roughly. (Pour boiling water over a bowl of tomatoes first to help loosen the skins if the skins are stubborn to remove.) Add all the peeled tomatoes to the pan with some vegetable or chicken stock and stir gently over a low heat until thoroughly cooked. If the soup appears to need more liquid, add a little more stock – or just plain water if there is no stock available. Don't add too much water or stock; better to turn down the heat a little rather than let the natural tomato juices evaporate away!

When cooked through, add a teaspoon or two of chopped fresh basil or other seasonal herbs and heat for another few minutes. Serve hot with a crusty loaf.

This soup can be blended just before serving if preferred and a spoonful of cream swirled into each bowlful as a special treat!

Potato and Leek Soup

Potatoes and leeks were, and still are, good solid standby vegetables during the winter months. A potato and leek soup is nourishing and wholesome and is filling enough to be a stand-alone meal. (Although bread is traditionally served with soup, potato-based soups tend to be very filling and are already full of carbo-hydrates!) The following recipe will serve 2–3 people.

Ingredients

    1lb (500g) potatoes
    2–3 leeks
    1–2 pints of chicken or vegetable stock
    a little cooking oil or butter
    seasoning – salt and pepper, fresh chopped herbs
    chopped chives or parsley to garnish – optional

Method

Peel and cut the potatoes into small pieces. Prepare the leeks: wash and remove outer leaves if they look a little rough then cut into thin slices. Gently heat oil or butter in a heavy-based large saucepan and cook the potatoes and leeks for a few minutes until they begin to soften. Stir with a wooden spoon and don't let the vegetables burn.

Add the stock to the pan with any seasoning you have available and bring to the boil. Reduce heat and simmer for at least 30 minutes. Cook until the potatoes are mushy or, alternatively, blend in a liquidiser or food processor as soon as the vegetables are tender. Serve hot. Garnish with a few chopped chives or a sprig of parsley.

Vegetable Soup

Vegetable soup can take on a new look at every sitting. Use the vegetables you have available to make a heart-warming and unique meal. Root vegetables are a good base for your soup then you can add any other bits and pieces you have to hand. Chopped cabbage or other green vegetables make a colourful addition as well as adding flavour, vitamins and minerals. Use a chicken or vegetable stock and be liberal with herbs to flavour your soup. Vegetable soups can be bland without a little seasoning. Salt and pepper may be added but don't use too much salt. The following recipe will be enough for 4 or 5 people.

Ingredients

     2 carrots
     a large turnip or 2 small ones
     1–2 sticks celery
     1 leek and/or 2 small onions
     1–2 parsnips
     half a small cabbage
     a few cauliflower florets
     a little butter or cooking oil
     vegetable or chicken stock
     seasoning
     1 or 2 bay leaves and/or a bouquet garni if available

NB: a bouquet garni is a bunch of herbs tied together with a natural string — make sure the string isn't one that will unravel or release small 'hairs' during cooking. The usual herbs to use would be bay leaves, thyme and parsley but any seasonal herbs can be used. If you wish to use dried herbs to flavour the dish, tie them in a small piece of muslin – remove either herb mix before serving.

Method

Peel and prepare all vegetables, cutting into small pieces for quicker cooking time. Sauté in a little butter or cooking oil in a large heavy-based saucepan until they start to soften. Keep on a low heat, stir and make sure the vegetables don't burn.

Add the stock and bay leaf or herbs and bring to the boil. Reduce heat and simmer until all vegetables are tender. Add seasoning – a little salt and pepper or a handful of mixed chopped herbs.

Remove the bay leaf or herbs before serving. Serve hot with a crusty loaf. If preferred, blend in a food processor or liquidiser and then reheat gently for a few minutes.

NB: this recipe is a guideline for vegetable soup – most vegetables can be added. A few tomatoes or even slices of green or red pepper could be used.

Pea Soup

Pea soup has often been used to describe London fog – thick and green! Well, maybe not quite so green – the main differences between London fog and pea soup are that pea soup is heart-warming, good for you and delicious. The same cannot be said for London fog!

Although pea soup isn't such a popular choice amongst soup eaters these days, it is a very tasty and nourishing meal and should be tried – at least once! Pea soup is best made with fresh peas but, out of season, split peas are just as good and dried split peas are always available to buy. The recipe below uses fresh peas but, to adapt it for dried peas, soak the peas for 12 hours before using and boil for 2 or 3 hours until tender.

Ingredients

about 2lb (900g) fresh shelled peas
a little butter or cooking oil
1 small onion, peeled and chopped
vegetable or chicken stock
seasoning
a handful of chopped fresh herbs – mint is the most compatible
    with pea soup but any seasonal herbs will do

Method

Cook the onion in the butter or cooking oil until soft. Use a large heavy-based saucepan. Add the peas, stock, seasoning and herbs and bring to the boil. Reduce heat and simmer for about 40 minutes until the peas are tender. Take off the heat and allow to cool slightly.

Blend in a food processor or blender until smooth. Reheat gently for a couple of minutes and serve hot.

Main Courses

Traditional Sunday Roast with Yorkshire Pudding

Now this was a meal all grannies seemed to be good at! But you don't have to be over sixty to qualify to make a traditional and delicious Sunday roast. Whether you choose to cook a joint of beef, pork, lamb, a chicken or turkey, or even a vegetarian nut roast, the Sunday dinner will set you up for the rest of the week! This meal is usually served around lunchtime-ish to allow everyone to take a walk – or a sleep in the afternoon. So starting early is essential.

Ingredients

      a joint of beef, a chicken or whatever you prefer
      potatoes
      green vegetables of choice – cauliflower, cabbage, broccoli etc
      carrots
      peas
      gravy powder
      cooking oil

Yorkshire puddings
> about 4oz (100g) plain flour
> 1 egg
> approx. ½ pint of milk

Traditional accompaniments
> with beef – horseradish sauce
> with lamb – mint sauce
> with pork – apple sauce
> with poultry or game – cranberry sauce or a sage-and-onion stuffing

You will also need a large baking dish, several saucepans and a patty tin for the Yorkshire puddings.

Method

Preheat the oven to the recommended temperature according to the meat you have bought. Prepare the meat, wash it and place in a baking dish with a little oil drizzled over the top.

Put it in the oven. Generally, it is recommended that meat be cooked around gas mark 5 (375F or 190C) for approximately 20–25 minutes per pound weight and then a further 20–25 minutes. However, a joint of meat or a chicken or turkey is often much tastier if cooked longer and slower. Reduce the heat to gas mark 4 (350F or 180C) and add another hour or more to the cooking time.

Prepare all vegetables. Peel and cut potatoes into 'roast-sized' pieces. Place in a saucepan, cover with water and bring to the boil. Boil for about 5–10 minutes; this is par-boiling – the potatoes aren't cooked but the outside has started to soften and will crisp nicely when placed in the oven later. Drain the potatoes and set aside.

Prepare green vegetables and place in a saucepan of water – or a steamer if you have one. Do the same with the carrots and peas.

Make the Yorkshire pudding batter. Pour about 4oz (100g) plain flour into a bowl and make a well in the centre. Break an egg into the well and add a little milk. Using a wooden spoon, stir the flour into the egg and milk and add more milk slowly, stirring all the time, until you have a thick, flowing batter. Keep in the fridge for about 30 minutes.

Prepare the sage and onion stuffing if using and set aside ready for baking.

Put plates in a warm place and lay the table. Remember the accompaniments and don't forget to uncork the wine!

Check the joint of meat from time to time and turn if necessary. Baste to keep the meat moist: using a large spoon, pour the cooking juices from the baking dish over the meat once or twice during cooking time.

When the meat has approximately another hour left to cook, put all the potatoes around it in the baking dish and return it to the oven.

Turn potatoes after half an hour. Make sure they are crisping. If not, turn the oven up a notch.

Put a tiny drop of oil or melted butter into each compartment in the patty tin or tins. Place in the oven for a couple of minutes to heat. Put the vegetables on to steam or boil. Remove patty tins and brush the oil to cover each part completely so the batter doesn't stick. Stir the Yorkshire pudding batter and pour a little into each compartment.

At this point, you will need to turn the oven up to almost its highest setting, so to avoid burning, place the meat in the lowest part of the oven, or remove and keep warm. Put the meat into another dish so you can keep the potatoes cooking in the same dish.

Put the Yorkshire puddings into the oven on the highest tray and also put the stuffing into the oven, if using. These two dishes will take approximately 20 minutes to cook through. Keep an eye on the Yorkshires so as not to burn them.

After about 10–15 minutes, start dishing up the meal. Put the potatoes into a warm serving dish and if you are making the gravy from the old-fashioned type gravy powder, pour off most off the fat from the cooking dish and add a table-spoon or two of gravy powder to the dish. Stir well, and slowly add water, stirring all the time. Put on to the heat and heat through gently – keep stirring to avoid lumps. Or, simply use gravy granules and prepare in a serving jug.

Carve the meat and place on to a warm serving plate or individual plates.

Drain vegetables and put into warm serving dishes, or directly on to plates if you are serving up a regular family meal. Remove the stuffing and Yorkshire puddings from the oven and finally turn the oven off! Bon appetit!

Tip: If you can get someone to help you in the last hour of cooking, clear up the kitchen as you go, wash up saucepans etc, or load the dishwasher. There's nothing worse than enjoying a wonderful meal, then facing a totally wrecked kitchen!

Shepherd's Pie

A traditional shepherd's pie would have been made with minced lamb – obvious I guess! But shepherd's or cottage pie can be made with minced beef or even soya mince. It's a great meal to make with Sunday roast leftovers – if you have any! An old-fashioned mincing machine will help prepare the cold meat or a blender will work just as well, although don't blend for too long – the meat needs to be like mince, not a paste.

If you have no leftover minced meat, use bought mince and cook thoroughly before using.

Tip: to cook mince and remove nearly all the fat, cover with water in a saucepan and bring to the boil. Put a lid on the saucepan, reduce the heat and simmer until the meat is cooked. Leave to cool completely. The fat from the meat will rise to the top of the water. When cold, the fat can be removed.

Ingredients

(serves 4)

8oz (200g) cooked minced meat, preferably beef or lamb, or vegetarian substitute

8oz (200g) boiled potatoes, drained

1 onion

a little seasoning

a knob of butter

a little milk

stock or gravy

Method

Preheat the oven to gas mark 4–5 (350–375F, 180–190C).

Mix the minced meat with the finely chopped onion. If you have a couple of soft tomatoes in the fridge, chop and mix them in as well. Season the mixture with a little salt and pepper or mixed herbs and put into a greased ovenproof dish. Pour over a little gravy or stock – not too much though – just enough to moisten the meat mixture, not to cover it.

Mash the boiled potatoes with a little butter and milk and spread on top of the meat. Smooth over then, using a fork, make a pattern on the top. Pop into the hot oven for about 30 minutes – until piping hot right through.

NB: always make sure re-heated meat dishes are thoroughly hot before serving.

For an extra special topping, grate some cheese over the potato after cooking and put under a moderate grill for 5 minutes or until golden brown.

Mariner's Pie

As the title suggests, mariner's pie is the fish version of shepherd's pie. The fish can be topped with sliced potatoes or mash, depending on your preference.

Use white fish and cook it beforehand: poaching in a saucepan of water is the best method. Cover the fish with water and add a little vinegar. Bring to the boil, reduce the heat and simmer for 5–15 minutes depending on the size of the fish.

Ingredients

> 1lb (500g) white fish, cooked and flaked – be careful to remove every bone
> 1lb (500g) peeled sliced potatoes, boiled (or steamed)
> 3 tablespoons of natural yoghurt or crème fraîche
> about 4–6oz (100–150g) mushrooms, sliced
> 2 hard-boiled eggs – optional
> handful of chopped parsley or a mixture of fresh seasonal herbs
> a little butter
> stock or water
> grated cheese

Method

Preheat the oven to gas mark 4 (350F, 180C)

Melt the butter in a pan and gently cook the mushrooms. Add the fish, yoghurt, herbs and a little stock or water and cook gently for a few minutes. Remove from heat. Peel and chop hard-boiled eggs if using, and stir into the fish mixture. Put the mixture into an ovenproof dish.

Arrange sliced boiled potatoes over the top or mash with a little milk and butter and spread over the mixture. Top with a little grated cheese and bake in the oven for about 30 minutes, or until hot right through. Serve immediately with green vegetables or a green salad.

Pie and Mash

All Londoners over a 'certain' age will remember pie and mash! This traditional dish had special eating places devoted to it and still does in a few locations in the East End of London. Pie and mash was served with what was called a parsley liquor, although it wasn't alcoholic – it was basically just a parsley sauce. The pastry and potatoes were very filling and of course brimming with carbs – but we didn't really know about carbs and stuff back then so it was even tastier and enjoyed by most Londoners!

Ingredients

> a packet of ready-made shortcrust pastry or, if you prefer to make your own, you will need:
>
> 8oz (200g) plain flour
>
> 4oz (100g) block margarine – originally a shortcrust pastry would have been made with half butter and half lard. But lard isn't always available, and there was a colossal amount of saturated fat in butter and lard
>
> a little cold water to mix

You will need a rolling pin as well – or a plastic smooth bottle full of dried beans or something similar. And a pie dish or individual pie dishes.

For the filling

> 1lb (500g) minced beef
>
> 1 onion
>
> a little cooking oil
>
> 4oz (100g) mushrooms
>
> 1 clove garlic
>
> 1 tablespoon tomato purée
>
> 1 teaspoon mustard – or according to taste
>
> about 10–12fl oz (300–350ml) beer – not lager
>
> 2 tablespoons of plain white flour

For the parsley liquor

> 4 tablespoons chopped fresh parsley
>
> 1oz (25g) butter
>
> 1oz (25g) plain white flour
>
> 10fl oz (300ml) vegetable or chicken stock (water can be used if no stock is available)
>
> seasoning

For the mash

> potatoes
>
> a little milk and a knob of butter

Method

Preheat the oven to gas mark 7 (425F or 220C).

Prepare the potatoes: peel and cut into fairly small pieces and cover with water in a saucepan.

Chop the onion, crush or finely chop the garlic and slice the mushrooms. Cook in a little cooking oil until the onion is soft, and then set aside. Brown the mince in the pan with a little oil and then stir in the flour and tomato purée. Cook for a few minutes. Add the onion, garlic, mushrooms and mustard and stir thoroughly. Pour in the beer and bring to the boil. Reduce heat and simmer for about 20 minutes. Remove from the heat and pour into a pie dish or individual dishes.

Roll out the bought pastry on a floured board. Or make your own by the following method.

Cut the cold block margarine into small pieces and add to the flour in a large bowl. Using the fingertips, rub the margarine into the flour to make a bread-crumb-type mix. Slowly add cold water – a very small amount at a time – and press the pastry together until firm but not sticky. If you do add a little too much water, knead in a little more flour. But to get the best results, add water a little at a time to avoid an over-sticky and heavy pastry.

Tip: for a lighter pastry, use only your fingertips to rub the margarine into the flour, and try to make sure your hands are cold.

On a floured board, roll out the pastry big enough to cover the pie dish or individual dishes. Cover the meat mixture with the pastry and brush with a little milk to glaze.

Put the pies in oven and bake for about 25–30 minutes, for one large one, or about 15 minutes, for small pies.

Bring the potatoes to the boil. Then reduce heat and simmer for about 20 minutes.

While the potatoes and pies are cooking, make the parsley sauce.

Melt the butter in a saucepan and stir in the flour. Cook for a minute on a very low heat, stirring and taking care not to burn. Then slowly add the stock or water and bring to the boil, stirring all the time. Add the parsley and seasoning (a little salt and black pepper to taste). Mix thoroughly and keep warm.

Drain and mash the potatoes with a knob of butter and a little milk. Remove the pies from the oven and serve at once with the mashed potatoes and parsley sauce.

Steak and Kidney Pudding

Steak and kidney pudding is made with a suet pastry and would have been bursting with calories in the old days! However, there is now available low-fat suet or vegetarian suet, both of which will be perfectly adequate to make a steak and kidney pudding. There may be a ready-made suet pastry available in your local supermarket if you prefer a quicker method, or a suet pastry mix which you simply add water to. The preparation time for this meal is fairly quick but the pudding will take about 5 hours to cook. You will need a 3-pint pudding basin, a large saucepan with a lid, and a plate that will fit into the bottom of the saucepan.

Ingredients

> 1½lb (675g) stewing steak, trimmed of fat and gristle and cut into small cubes
> 8oz (200g) ox kidney, trimmed and cut into small cubes
> 1 medium onion, finely chopped
> a little less than ¼ pint or 120ml water or beef stock
> seasoning – salt and black pepper
> 2 tbsp plain flour

For the suet pastry

> 12oz (350g) self-raising flour – or plain flour mixed with with 2 teaspoons of baking powder
> 6oz (150g) beef or vegetarian shredded suet
> margarine to grease basin

> You will also need greaseproof paper, aluminium foil and string.

Method

Mix together the steak, kidney, onion, seasoning and 2 tbsp of plain flour in a bowl. Stir well, to ensure all ingredients are coated with the flour.

To make the pastry

Mix together the flour and suet and a pinch of salt. Add water a little at a time, mixing until a soft dough is formed. Knead and roll out into a circle about 14in (35cm) across on a floured board. Cut out a quarter of the dough for the lid and set aside.

Lightly grease a basin with the margarine and line with the pastry. Seal well and leave about an inch of pastry overlapping at the top.

Spoon the meat mix into the pastry-lined basin and spread evenly. Add about 120ml of water. The water should not come to the top of the mixture.

Roll out the set aside quarter of dough to about an inch larger than the top of the basin. Lift on to the basin and seal the edges around the top with water.

Butter one side of a circle of greaseproof paper and lay on top of the pastry. Then cover with a layer of aluminium foil, pleated in the middle and sealed around the edge of the basin. The pleat is to allow for expansion during cooking time.

Bring a very large saucepan of water to the boil. Place an upturned plate in the bottom before it gets hot. While the water is heating up, make a string handle for the basin, tied round the top of the basin and loose at the top so as to be able to lift from the saucepan later. Then when the water is boiling, put the basin on to the plate, upright, and cover saucepan with a lid. Steam the pudding for 5 hours. Check from time to time on the water level. The pan must not boil dry. Top up with boiling water so that the water does not go off the boil at all.

To serve, uncover, garnish with a sprig of parsley if required and serve with mashed potatoes and peas.

Steak and Kidney Pie

Similar to a steak and kidney pudding but oh so very different! Steak and kidney pie can be made with shortcrust or puff pastry, and can easily turn into a family mid-week special. Add peas or sliced mushrooms or spice it up a little with a spoonful of curry powder. This recipe is a traditional steak and kidney pie made with shortcrust pastry and will serve four people. You will need a 2-pint pie dish and a large saucepan.

Ingredients

> 1½lb (675g) stewing steak, trimmed of fat and gristle and cut into small cubes
> 8oz (200g) ox kidney, trimmed and cut into small cubes
> 1 medium onion, sliced
> about ¾ pint or 450ml water or beef stock
> seasoning – salt and black pepper
> 2 tbsp plain flour
> 1 beaten egg to glaze

For the pastry
> 8oz (200g) plain flour
> 4oz (100g) block margarine – or half lard and half margarine
> cold water

Method

Coat cubes of meat with the plain flour – season the flour first if preferred – and put into the saucepan with the sliced onion and stock. Bring to the boil, reduce heat and cover with lid. Simmer for 1½–2 hours until meat is tender. Season. (If preferred, the meat can be cooked in a casserole dish in the oven for 2 hours at gas mark 3 (325F or 170C).)

Allow to cool completely and then chill for a while in the fridge until very cold. Preheat oven to gas mark 7 (425F or 220C)

Make the pastry: cut the margarine into small pieces and rub into the flour with fingertips until the mixture resembles breadcrumbs. Add water very slowly, mixing all the time until a firm dough is produced. Roll out on to a floured board until the pastry is slightly larger than the top of the pie dish.

Put the meat mixture into the dish and cover with the circle of pastry. Stick it to the dish with water. With the trimmings, cut a half-inch strip and double up the edge of the pastry all round, sealing with a little water. Use your fingertip dipped in cold water to stick the two edges together. With any trimmings left, make a leaf shape and stick to the top of the pie. Make a couple of 1-inch slits with a knife in the centre of the lid to allow steam to escape.

Brush with beaten egg to glaze.

Bake in the preheated oven for 20 minutes then reduce heat to gas mark 4 (350F or 180C) and cook for another 20 minutes.

Serve with mashed potatoes and green vegetables, or just the green vegetables if you are cutting carbs!

Boiled Beef and Carrots

This is a very well-known and easy-to-make family dinner – and it's nourishing as well, especially in the colder months of the year. There's even been a song written about boiled beef and carrots, although that's the only line I can recall so I won't sing it just now! Traditionally a London recipe, boiled beef and carrots is one of the tastiest combinations of foods that have survived the test of time. Sadly, we don't often make the dish as beef is rather more expensive than it used to be, pro rata. However, a cheaper cut of beef when boiled for a fair amount of time will become tender enough to melt in the mouth. Use a large saucepan and definitely try out the dumplings!

Ingredients

2½lb (1–1.5kg) of brisket of beef or silver side
3–4 pints (2 litres) of stock
2 small turnips
1–2 medium-sized onions
16–20 small carrots or larger ones cut in half
1 bouquet garni (or make your own using seasonal herbs tied into a bunch or dried herbs tied into a small piece of muslin)
1–2 bay leaves

For the dumplings

    4oz (100g) self-raising flour (or plain flour with 1–2 tsp of baking powder)
    2oz (50g.) shredded suet
    cold water
    finely chopped parsley – optional

Method

Tie the joint of meat with string or, if preferred (and to reduce cooking time), cut meat into small pieces. Put meat into saucepan and cover with stock. Bring to the boil.

Prepare the turnips and onions and cut into small pieces. Add to the saucepan with the herbs and simmer for a couple of hours or less if you have cut the meat up. Keep an eye on the level of liquid, adding more hot stock if necessary.

Prepare the carrots and add to the pan. Cook for a further 30–40 minutes until carrots are tender.

Dumplings

Mix the flour and shredded suet in a bowl and add the parsley, if using. Slowly add cold water until an elastic dough is formed. Using floured hands, roll into about 16 small balls.

Drop carefully into the saucepan about 20 minutes before the end of the cooking time.

Remove the meat, carrots and dumplings carefully and keep warm in a serving dish. Boil the remaining stock rapidly for a few minutes. Liquidise or blend in a food blender for a few seconds, or put through a sieve. Then pour into a gravy jug.

Serve hot with mashed or boiled potatoes and green vegetables.

Snacks

Poached Eggs on Toast

Poached eggs on toast can be eaten for breakfast, lunch or a light evening meal. A poacher can be used to poach the eggs but before poachers were invented, poached eggs were even tastier. This is a recipe to demonstrate how poached eggs were poached in days of old. Fish can be poached in this way as well. You will need a small to medium-sized saucepan. Use a small one for 1 egg or a medium saucepan for 2 eggs.

Ingredients

      eggs – allow 1–2 per person
      sliced bread – allow 1–2 slices per person
      butter or margarine for spreading
      malt vinegar

Method

Half fill your saucepan with cold water and bring to the boil. Pour in about 1 tbsp of malt vinegar, and lower the heat to simmering point. Break the eggs into a cup or small bowl, making sure you remove bits of broken shell. Pour the eggs gently from the bowl into the simmering water, taking care not to break the yolks.

Bring the water back to the boil, reduce the heat again and simmer for a few minutes until the white of the egg is firm.

While the egg is cooking, put bread into the toaster or under the grill and lightly toast on both sides. Spread with a little butter or margarine and put on to a warm plate.

When the eggs are cooked, remove from the water with a slotted spoon, drain for a few seconds and carefully place on to the toast. Serve hot.

Welsh Rarebit

Welsh rarebit is an extra-special version of cheese on toast and can even be made with brown ale but, if cooking for the kids, it's probably best to stick to milk! This is a perfect protein-rich snack and can be eaten as a main meal served with a poached egg on top, or grilled bacon or ham, and with a green salad. Tomatoes are always a good accompaniment to cheese and slices of grilled tomato will bring out the flavours, as will chopped spring onions. This recipe tells how to make a basic Welsh rarebit sauce. Add whatever you have available in the fridge to zap it up a bit!

Ingredients

8oz (200g) hard cheese, grated
1oz (25g) butter or margarine
1 tsp mustard powder or 2 tsp of a milder ready-made mustard
a little salt and black pepper for seasoning
4 tbsp brown ale or milk
4 slices of bread

Method

Put all ingredients – except for the bread – into a saucepan and cook gently until a creamy mixture is formed. Stir continuously to avoid the mixture sticking to the pan. Toast one side of the bread and place on to warm plates, uncooked side up. Pour over the sauce and eat while hot.

Garnish with a few chopped spring onions, chives, grilled slices of tomatoes, or even slices of green pepper, if required.

Fish Cakes

Fish cakes are easily available in any frozen food department of almost every supermarket but home-made fish cakes are far tastier and more fun and you have control over the quality and amount of fish you are putting into them.

Ingredients

8oz (200g) cooked white fish (e.g. cod or haddock), allowed to go cold
8oz (200g) boiled potatoes
1 egg
about 3oz (75g) fresh breadcrumbs
a little butter

a little milk
a little flour
salt and pepper
chopped fresh seasonal herbs – optional
oil for frying

Method

Flake the fish and remove all skin and bones. Be very careful to remove every bone. Put the fish into a large bowl.

Mash the boiled potatoes with the milk and butter until smooth. Mix together the fish, mashed potatoes, a little salt and pepper and herbs, if using.

With a little flour, form into small cakes. Beat the egg in a bowl and spread the breadcrumbs on a board or large plate. Dip each cake into the beaten egg then roll in the breadcrumbs. Fry in hot oil for a few minutes on each side until hot right through.

Serve hot or cold with a green salad.

Rissoles

Rissoles are a tasty way of serving minced beef or you could use a vegetarian substitute. Experiment with the ingredients. Add a little curry powder or even chilli sauce if you like hot and spicy. Or mix in some cooked split peas or lentils, if available. This recipe will make about 8 rissoles and can be served as a main meal with potatoes, green vegetables and gravy, or with a green salad. Mashed potato can be mixed in with the meat mixture before cooking to add bulk.

Ingredients

about 1lb (500g) minced beef, cooked and cooled
1–2 medium onions, finely chopped
3–4oz (75–100g) plain flour
2 eggs
salt and pepper
oil for frying

Method

Cook the minced beef (see p. 26 for tip on how to remove fat from mince).

Mix together, in a large bowl, the cooked mince, onions, salt and pepper, half the flour and any other ingredients you are using.

Beat one egg and mix well to bind the mixture together. If the mixture is still too dry to stick together, add a little stock or another beaten egg.

Form the meat mixture into burger shapes. Beat the other egg in a bowl and dip each rissole into the egg to coat thoroughly. Put the rest of the flour on to a board or a large plate and roll each rissole in the flour. Season the flour first, if you want to, using a few dried herbs or salt and pepper.

Fry rissoles in hot oil for a few minutes each side until they are hot right through. When re-heating meat, always make sure the meat is piping hot before serving.

Desserts

Apple Pie

Apple pie is just about a universal dessert. Is there anyone who hasn't tasted it at least once in their life? If you enjoy baking and making pastry, an apple pie is a great standby dessert for the family. It's inexpensive and would have been made with cooking apples only during years gone by. It can be made with everyday dessert apples but you will get a better result using cooking apples. If you have an apple tree in your garden, use the windfalls – takes a little time, but hey, it's good to have time to think sometimes!

Ingredients
     2lb (900g) cooking apples
     2oz (50g) white or brown sugar
     1 beaten egg for glazing – optional

12oz (300g) ready-made shortcrust pastry or, to make your own, you will
    need:
8oz (200g) plain flour
4oz (100g) block margarine – or half margarine and half lard
cold water

You will also need a 2-pint pie dish.

Method
Preheat the oven to gas mark 6 (400F or 200C).

Peel and core the apples and slice very finely. Put into the pie dish and sprinkle
the sugar over the top. If you are using cooking apples, you may want to pre-cook
them a little first. Put the sliced apple into a saucepan and cover with a little
water. Bring to the boil, reduce the heat and simmer for a few minutes until
starting to soften. Drain and place in the pie dish.

Make the pastry. Ensure the margarine is very cold. Cut into pieces and rub
into the flour using the fingertips, until the mixture resembles breadcrumbs. Your
hands should not be too warm. The cooler the ingredients, the lighter the pastry.
Add cold water a little at a time to form a soft dough.

Roll the pastry out on a floured board until large enough to cover the pie
dish. Place over the dish and seal with water. Brush with beaten egg to glaze if
preferred.

Bake in the preheated oven for about 30–40 minutes until the pastry is golden
brown. Remove and allow to cool for a few minutes. Sprinkle with a little caster
sugar if liked.

Serve hot or cold, on its own or with custard or cream.

Blackberry and Apple Crumble

The wonderful hours you can spend avoiding wasps while picking blackberries!
Wear a pair of gardening gloves to protect your hands from the thorns as well as
the wasps. But, aside from the dangers, you really must try a fresh blackberry and
apple crumble, if you never have. A truly wonderful experience! Pick blackberries
fresh if you can, but avoid those by the side of the road (car pollution) or very low
growing fruits (dog pollution). If there are none to be found, buy them, or even
better, buy a shrub to plant in the garden so you have some available every year.

Ingredients
    2lb (900g) cooking or dessert apples
    2oz (50g) white or brown sugar

blackberries – enough for at least one layer over your apples, but more if you can find them

Crumble mix
>6oz (150g) plain flour
>3oz (75g) block margarine
>3oz (75g) caster sugar

You will also need a 2-pint pie dish.

Method
Preheat the oven to gas mark 5 (375F or 190C).

Peel and core the apples and slice finely. Put into the pie dish and sprinkle sugar over the top. Cooking apples can be sliced and pre-cooked for a few minutes in a saucepan, before adding to the pie dish.

Prepare the blackberries by gently washing them and removing any stalks etc. Add them to the apples in the dish.

Make the crumble mix. Cut the block margarine into small pieces – make sure it is fairly cold. Then rub into the flour with your fingertips, until the mixture resembles fine breadcrumbs. Add a little more flour if the mix seems a bit sticky. Then stir in the sugar.

Pile the crumble mix on top of the fruit and bake in the oven for about half an hour, or until the top of the crumble is looking lightly browned.

Serve hot with custard, cream or on its own. Keep any remaining portion in the fridge as it can be eaten cold the next day.

Eve's Pudding

Eve's pudding was traditionally made in late summer when the apples were ready to be harvested. But it can be made any time of the year of course, and is also just as delicious made with apricots or even pears. If you like sponge cakes and fruit you will love an Eve's Pudding! It can be made with dessert apples as well as cooking apples. Cooking apples need to be stewed a little beforehand, but dessert apples are soft enough as they are. You will need a 1½-pint ovenproof dish.

Ingredients
>1lb (450g) cooking apples or dessert apples
>1oz (25g) white or brown sugar
>a little lemon juice
>a little margarine to grease dish

Topping

 5oz (150g) self-raising flour or plain flour with 2 tsp of baking powder
 3oz (75g) block margarine
 3oz (75g) caster sugar
 1 large egg, beaten
 a little milk – or use 2 medium beaten eggs instead of milk, if preferred

Method

Preheat the oven to gas mark 4 (350F or 180C). Lightly grease a pie dish.

Peel and core the apples and slice thinly. If using cooking apples, put into a saucepan with a little water and the lemon juice and bring to the boil. Reduce heat and simmer for about 5 minutes to soften the apples. Leave to cool.

If using dessert apples, slice thinly and place into a prepared pie dish. Pour over a little lemon juice and about 1oz (25g) of sugar. Add a touch more if you feel the apples are a little sharp tasting.

Make the topping. Cream the margarine and sugar together with a wooden spoon or a food mixer until light and fluffy. Add the beaten egg, a little at a time, beating well after each addition. Fold in the flour with a metal spoon. The mixture needs to be of a 'dropping' consistency, so if it doesn't fall slowly from the spoon, add a little milk.

Spread the topping over the fruit and bake in the oven for about 45 minutes, until the apples are tender and the topping is golden brown.

Dust with a little sugar if liked.

Serve hot with custard or cream, or on its own. Eve's Pudding will keep for several days in the fridge and can be eaten cold.

Rhubarb and Custard

Rhubarb was often grown in the back garden and although officially a vegetable, the stems are always used in sweet dishes. (Never eat the leaves of rhubarb – they are poisonous.) Choose the smaller pinker stems if possible as the larger ones tend to be more acidic and sharper tasting. Rhubarb can also be used in crumble recipes or pies, but rhubarb and custard was a very popular standby family pudding. Make your own custard if you can be bothered, or use a ready-made packaged favourite. Always thoroughly cook rhubarb. It's not a food to be eaten raw!

Ingredients

 2lb (1kg) fresh rhubarb
 6oz (150g) sugar – brown sugar or less processed sugars are best
 water

Home-made custard

      (makes ½ pint of custard)

      ½ pint (300ml) milk

      2 eggs

      1–2oz (25–50g) caster or granulated white sugar

      ½ a split vanilla pod – optional. You can also use a few thin strips of lemon
         rind for flavouring

Method

Prepare the rhubarb. Wash and trim and cut into 1-inch lengths. Put into a pan with the sugar and a little water. Bring to the boil. Reduce the heat and simmer for about 10 minutes or until the rhubarb is tender. Stir every now and then or gently shake the pan. Strain the rhubarb and serve in warmed bowls.

Make the custard while the rhubarb is cooking. In a bowl, beat the eggs, sugar and about 3 tbsp of milk together until smooth. Put the rest of the milk into a saucepan with the vanilla pod or lemon rind. Bring to the boil slowly. Remove from the heat. Put a lid on the saucepan and leave for ten minutes to absorb the flavouring. Remove the vanilla pod if used.

Pour the milk on to the egg mixture and then strain the mixture into a heavy-based saucepan. Cook gently on a low heat until the custard thickens to the required consistency. Do not boil. Pour into a jug or directly on to your dessert.

Trifle

Trifle is a perfect summer dessert. Chilled and served on its own, it contains just about every sweet item you can think of! Make your own unique recipe by adding a little sherry or a liqueur if feeding over eighteens. The following recipe is a traditional old English recipe but to make a quick and easy trifle you can simply place some trifle sponges and a tin of fruit cocktail in the bottom of a dish. Make a jelly and pour over the top. When set, add a layer of prepared blancmange and then a layer of custard and top it with some whipped cream.

Start the preparation early in the day whichever recipe you use, as you need to wait for the separate layers to set or marinate before adding another. A large glass serving dish is perfect for a trifle.

Ingredients

      1 pint (600ml) milk

      2 eggs + 2 egg yolks

      1–2oz (25–50g) caster or granulated white sugar

½ a split vanilla pod – optional. You can also use a few thin strips of lemon rind for flavouring

1 sponge cake or 8 trifle sponges

6oz (175g) strawberry jam – or any preferred flavour

3–4 fl oz (100ml) sherry or a light rum or liqueur

10fl oz (300ml) double or whipping cream

small chocolate flakes, glacé cherries or other crystallised fruits (for decoration)

Method

Make the custard following the home-made custard recipe, described under 'rhubarb and custard', adding the extra egg yolks for a richer custard. When made, leave to cool. Sprinkle a little sugar over the top to prevent a skin forming. If a skin does form, remove with a spoon or knife. Leave until completely cold.

Cut the sponge cake into pieces, or use the trifle sponges. Spread the jam on each piece and place in a serving dish. Spoon over the sherry and leave to marinate for a couple of hours. Pour the cold custard over the sponge. Then whip the cream and spread over the custard. Decorate as required.

Victoria Sandwich

A Victoria sandwich cake is the perfect sponge cake. If you make it by hand it takes a strong wrist and a little time but it's well worth the effort. If you have a food mixer, so much the better. Give it a go. You'll get loads of brownie points for this one! You need 2 sandwich tins (7in or 18cm), a large mixing bowl and a wooden spoon or a food mixer.

Ingredients

6oz (175g) self-raising flour or plain flour with 2 tsp of baking powder

6oz (175g) softened block margarine or butter

6oz (175g) caster sugar

3 medium eggs

Filling

3–4 tbsp jam and or butter icing

Butter-icing filling

4oz (100g) icing sugar

2oz (50g) softened butter

You will also need a little margarine for greasing and some greaseproof paper.

Method

Beat eggs in a basin. Grease sandwich tins and place a circle of greaseproof paper in the base of each. Sprinkle a little flour on to the greaseproof paper. Preheat oven to gas mark 5 (375F or 190C).

In a large bowl, and with a wooden spoon, beat the butter and caster sugar together until pale and fluffy. Use a food mixer for this if you have one available. Add the eggs a little at a time and beat well after each addition.

Using a metal spoon add half the flour and fold into the mixture. Then add the rest of the flour, and stir gently.

Spread the mixture between both tins and level off. Bake in the oven for about 20 minutes until they are firm to the touch, well risen and starting to shrink away from the sides of the tins. Leave for a minute or two and then turn on to a wire rack to cool completely.

To make a butter-icing filling

Beat together the sieved icing sugar and softened butter until pale and fluffy. A food mixer can be used to do this as well but make sure the bowl has been cleaned of the sponge mix first. When cakes are completely cool, sandwich the two halves together with jam and the butter icing. Dredge a little caster or icing sugar over the top if desired.

Fruit Cake

There are all sorts of fruit cakes, from a rich Christmas cake to a simple sultana sponge. This recipe takes us all the way to the Christmas tea table and way beyond into January! There are so many variations of a regular Christmas cake and as long as you get the basic texture right before cooking, you can't really go too far wrong. Soaking dried fruit in rum for a few days gives the cake a Jamaican flavour. And adding a small glass of brandy will help to preserve the cake, although the fruit and sugar will do that on their own (but you have an excuse – it's Christmas!). This recipe needs a round 9-inch (23cm) cake tin and will produce a 6lb (2.7kg) cake (approximately). You will need a very large mixing bowl, another slightly smaller one and a couple of basins, some string, brown paper, and greaseproof paper.

Ingredients

2lb 12oz (1¼ kilos) of mixed dried fruit – sultanas, glacé cherries, currants and raisins

4oz (100g) dried mixed peel

4oz (100g) finely chopped or flaked almonds, without peel

the rind of about ½ a lemon – buy a non-waxed variety, organic or wash well before use

2 level tsp mixed spice or cinnamon or a mixture of both

2–3 tbsp brandy

6 eggs

14oz (400g) plain flour

12oz (350g) block margarine (or butter)

12oz (350g) sugar – soft brown if available

Method

Preheat oven to gas mark 2 (300F or 150C). Prepare the cake tin: grease and line with two layers of greaseproof paper. Then tie a double layer of brown paper around the outside of the tin with string.

Prepare fruit: wash and dry if necessary and chop any over-large pieces – cherries, for example, are better halved or quartered. Mix together in a large bowl with the almonds and mixed peel.

In the largest bowl, cream together the butter, lemon rind and sugar until pale and fluffy. Beat the eggs into a small basin and add them, a little at a time, to the creamed mixture. Beat well after each addition.

Slowly fold in all the flour using a metal spoon then stir in the brandy.

Then add the fruit mix to the bowl and stir thoroughly. Everyone should stir the cake and make a wish at this point – according to tradition anyway!

Put the cake mixture into the prepared tin and spread evenly. Then with the back of a spoon make a gentle dip in the centre. This will ensure the cake has an even surface when cooked.

Stand the cake tin on brown paper in the oven and leave to cook for about 4 hours. Cover the top with greaseproof paper after about an hour and a half to prevent the top from burning.

Check the cake is cooked by inserting a skewer into the centre. If it comes out clean, then the cake is cooked right through. If not, leave for a further 30 minutes and check again.

Remove the cake from the oven when finished cooking and leave in the tin to cool. Then turn out on to a wire rack. Prick with a fine skewer all over the top of the cake and pour a little brandy over the whole thing. When completely cool and dry, wrap in greaseproof paper and store in a cake tin until required.

Fruit cakes improve their flavour with keeping so it's a good idea to make the cake at least a month before Christmas or whatever event you are making it for.

The fruit cake can be served as it is or covered with rolled-out marzipan and iced with royal or fondant icing.

To do this, you should first warm a little apricot jam and spread over the top and sides of the cake. Roll out marzipan on a board coated lightly in icing sugar. Place over the cake and leave to dry for 24 hours.

If you wish to make your own marzipan – or almond paste – you will need:

      1lb (450g) castor sugar or 8oz (225g) each of icing sugar and castor sugar
      1lb (450g) ground almonds
      2 eggs, beaten well
      flavouring: a few drops of almond or vanilla essence, or 1 tbsp of rose water

Stir together the sugars and ground almonds. Add the flavouring and then add the beaten eggs. Turn on to a board lightly dusted with icing sugar and knead the paste well together before rolling out and covering the cake.

Then buy or make the icing. To make royal icing – a hard icing, traditionally used on Christmas and wedding cakes – you will need:

      2lb (900g) icing sugar, sieved
      4 egg whites
      1 tbsp lemon juice
      2 tsp glycerine

The egg whites should be whisked until a little frothy. Stir in a quarter of the icing sugar then add all but the last quarter a little at a time, beating well after each addition.

Beat in the lemon juice and beat for a further 10 minutes until very smooth. Do this in the food mixer if you have one. It makes your wrist ache for days otherwise!

Then beat in the rest of the icing sugar until the consistency you want is achieved. Stir in the glycerine. Cover and keep for 24 hours before using. Then use to coat the cake. Smooth over the top and sides and, if preferred, rough up the surface by 'picking up' the icing gently with the back of a knife. Decorate with coloured marzipan or bought Christmas trees or other decorations.

Drinks

Dandelion and Burdock

Dandelion and burdock was made as a cordial, a beer and even a wine in gener-ations past. It can still be bought as a soft fizzy drink today, although how much of the original dandelion or burdock ingredients the modern-day drink contains is anyone's guess! Some recipes call for the root of the dandelion plant and others use the leaves. This one uses the roots only so, if you need to remove the dandelions from your garden, dig them up and put them to good use!

Ingredients

> 1 burdock root
> 2 dandelion roots
> 1lb (500g) granulated sugar
> 2 tbsp treacle
> juice of 1 lemon
> 1 tsp brewers' yeast
> 1 gallon of water

You will also need:
> soft-drink bottles with caps – enough to hold a gallon (8 pints or about 4 litres of fluid)
> a sterilised bucket with a cover – use a white plastic or stainless steel bucket

Method

Scrub the roots well and chop into small pieces. Put into a large saucepan with about 3 pints of the water and bring to the boil. Boil gently for about 20 minutes. Remove from the heat. Stir in the sugar and treacle until dissolved. Then mix in the lemon juice.

Strain into the bucket and make up to a gallon with water. Add the yeast and stir.

Cover the bucket and leave to ferment for 4 days. Then bottle in plastic bottles and leave for a further week. The bottles should be checked every couple of days for 'fizz'. Release the cap lightly if you think it may fizz over! But the drink will start to go flat when you do this, so it should be drunk straight away.

Elderberry Wine

Elderberries grow everywhere in the British countryside and in many moderate climates. The elder tree produces flowers that can be made into elderflower champagne and if the flowers aren't used they produce berries which have always traditionally been used to make a wine. A syrup can be made from the berries as well to provide a cordial to be diluted for children.

Ingredients
 3lb (1½kg) elderberries
 3lb (1½kg) sugar
 1–2 lemons
 1lb sultanas
 a little ground ginger or fresh bruised ginger
 ½oz yeast

You will also need:
 a fermenting bucket
 sterilised bottles
 demijohn

Method

Prepare the fruit. Remove stalks and other plant residue from the elderberries. A fork works well for this task. Mash the berries well or blend in a food processor or liquidiser for a minute or two.

 Put the mashed berries into a sterilised fermenting bucket and add a gallon of boiling water. Stir well and add the sultanas. Cover the bucket and leave for 4 days to ferment.

 Strain into a clean basin and then tip the liquid back into the bucket. Add the sugar and stir until dissolved. Then mix in the lemon juice and add the ginger. If using fresh ginger, bruise and place in a small muslin bag before adding to the bucket. Sprinkle the yeast over the liquid, cover and leave for a further 3 days.

 Strain again, removing the bag of ginger if used, and pour into a demijohn. Fix the airlock and leave in a cool place until the bubbling completely stops. At least four months should be allowed. After the bubbling has stopped, bottle and label.

This wine can be made in the summer, as soon as the elderberries are ripe, and will be ready in time to drink at Christmas.

Rosehip Syrup

Rosehips were collected in the war years in the UK from wild plants that grew all over the countryside. The government suggested recipes and encouraged everyone to collect rosehips to make a healthy syrup for growing children. Rosehip syrup was the best source of vitamin C available during the years when food was scarce. And the taste still lingers. Many of us who are not old enough to remember the war years will nevertheless remember the unforgettable taste of rosehip syrup.

Ingredients
    2lb (1kg) rosehips
    1lb (500g) preserving sugar

You will also need:
    2 large bowls
    a large heavy-based saucepan
    a jelly bag – a fine muslin bag to strain the syrup (or use a piece of muslin
        and a colander)
    glass bottles, sterilised

Method
Boil about 3 pints of water in a large saucepan. Wash then crush the rosehips and carefully add to the boiling water. Bring back to the boil then remove from the heat and leave to stand for 10 minutes. Strain the mixture through the jelly bag into a large bowl until it has stopped dripping. Then put the fruit back into a saucepan and add about 1½ pints of fresh boiling water. Bring back to the boil then remove from the heat and leave to stand. Strain the mixture through the jelly bag again into the other large bowl.

Now mix the two bowls of juice together into a clean pan. Bring to the boil and boil until the liquid has reduced to about 1½ pints. Reduce the heat and stir in the sugar until dissolved. Boil for a further 5 minutes.

Pour into hot glass sterilised bottles and seal. Keep in a cool dark place until required.

Blackcurrant Juice

Another wonderful source of vitamin C, practically all the commercially grown blackcurrants in the UK today go to make blackcurrant juice. You will need a fair few shrubs in the garden to produce enough blackcurrants for making quantities of juice, but even if you only have enough for a small amount, it's worth trying. This recipe makes a syrup that can be diluted to make a drink or poured over desserts as a sauce.

Ingredients

    4lbs (1.8kg) blackcurrants
    grated rind and juice of 2 oranges
    2 pints (1 litre) water
    1½lbs (675g) any white sugar

You will also need:
    a jelly bag or a piece of muslin and a colander
    a large heavy-based saucepan
    a large bowl
    a measuring jug
    glass bottles, sterilised, or mixture can be frozen in suitable freezer containers

Method

Prepare the fruit: wash and remove any stalks and leaves. Put the blackcurrants into a large pan with the water, orange juice and rind. Bring to the boil, stirring constantly and boil for about 2 minutes. Remove from the heat.

Crush the blackcurrants with a wooden spoon or potato masher then strain through a jelly bag or muslin and a colander into a bowl.

Pour the juice into a measuring jug then weigh 12oz (350g) sugar per pint of juice. Put the juice back into the pan, add the sugar and reheat gently until the sugar has dissolved.

Pour the juice into hot sterilised jars and seal. Or cool completely and freeze in freezer containers; even ice cube trays will do!

The syrup can be used to pour over desserts or diluted and drunk as a juice.

Jams and Pickles

Raspberry Jam

Raspberry jam can be made from home-produced raspberries. Buying them will make the jam very costly. Growing raspberries is easy and they will crop year after year when they get going. The more raspberries you produce the more jam can be made. Home-made jams make a wonderful gift, especially at Christmas time. And jam you've made yourself brings a wonderful taste of summer to your toast on the coldest of winter mornings!

Ingredients

> (makes about 6½lb or 3kg of jam)
> 4lb (1.8kg) raspberries
> 4lb (1.8kg) preserving sugar

You will also need:
> sterilised jars
> a large heavy-based saucepan
> sugar thermometer (see note below for setting point if you haven't got a sugar thermometer)

Method

Wash the fruit and remove any stalks, leaves or damaged parts. Drain well. Put all the fruit into the saucepan. Bring to the boil, then reduce the heat and simmer gently for about 20 minutes. Stir every now and then to prevent sticking or burning. When the fruit is very soft remove from the heat and stir in the sugar. Keep stirring until all the sugar is completely dissolved.

Return to the heat and boil rapidly for 30 minutes. Test for the setting point by inserting thermometer into the jam. The temperature must be 221°F or 105°C before removing from the heat. Using a metal spoon, take any scum from the surface and leave to stand for about 15 minutes. Spoon the jam into hot sterilised jars. Leave to cool, seal and label. Make sure the jars are hot before putting hot jam into them or they may crack.

Tip: if you haven't got a sugar thermometer, you can test for a set by dropping a very small amount of jam onto a cold saucer. After about 30 seconds to 1 minute, gently rub your finger or a spoon over the surface of the jam. If it wrinkles and appears to have produced a skin, the setting point has been reached.

Strawberry Jam

Strawberries can often be bought relatively cheaply these days and can be used for making jam. However, many will not be organic and will possibly not taste very much like home-grown strawberries. Get a strawberry patch going if you can, then protect from birds, pets and children if you want enough to make a jar of jam or more!

Ingredients
(makes about 5lb or 2.3kg of jam)
3lbs (1.4kg) strawberries
3lbs (1.4kg) preserving sugar
juice of half a lemon

You will also need:
sterilised jars
a large heavy-based saucepan
sugar thermometer (see note under raspberry jam for setting point if you haven't got a sugar thermometer)

Method
Wash the fruit and remove any stalks, leaves or damaged parts. Drain well. Put all the fruit and lemon juice into the saucepan. Bring to the boil, then reduce the heat and simmer gently for about 20–30 minutes. Stir every now and then to prevent sticking or burning. When the fruit is very soft, remove from the heat and stir in the sugar. Keep stirring until all the sugar is completely dissolved.

Return to the heat and boil rapidly for 20 minutes. Test for the setting point by inserting a thermometer into the jam. The temperature must be 221°F or 105°C before removing from heat. Using a metal spoon, remove any scum from the surface and leave to stand for about 15 minutes. Spoon the jam into hot sterilised jars. Leave to cool, seal and label. Make sure the jars are hot before putting hot jam into them or they may crack. Broken glass and hot jam all over the kitchen is not a particularly enjoyable scenario!

Pickled Onions

Pickled onions are always a family favourite, especially at Christmas time. Buy pickling onions especially for the job. They are small and will be crisp enough to keep for many months. You could grow them but the space in the garden would be better used for larger onions for everyday use. Pickling vinegar can be bought ready to use nowadays, but before it was available, malt vinegar would have been used and different spices added and left to marinate. The spices used could have included any or all of the following:

> black peppercorns
> blade mace
> cloves
> cinnamon sticks
> whole allspice

If you want to make your own pickling vinegar, add the spices to a bottle of vinegar. Leave for a few days before using for your onions.

The following recipe uses already spiced vinegar.

Ingredients
> 4lb (1.8kg) pickling onions
> 2 pints (1.1 litres) pickling vinegar

You will also need suitable jars, sterilised, or use the jar in which the pickling vinegar was bought if suitable.

Method
Peel all the onions and rinse. Drain well and pack into a sterilised jar. Pour over the vinegar, to almost fill the jars and seal with vinegar-proof lids. Label.

Pickled Eggs

A good old-fashioned solid way of keeping eggs! Use a white vinegar and make your own spice mixture from the above list. Add a crushed bay leaf if liked. The eggs should be kept for at least 6 weeks before using.

Ingredients

> 6 eggs
> About 1oz (25g) pickling spice mix (see above)
> 1 pint (600ml) white vinegar (cider or white wine)
> 4–6 cloves of garlic

You will also need a large wide-mouthed glass jar, with a vinegar-proof lid.

Method

Boil the eggs for 10 minutes. Peel and put into a bowl of cold water to cool completely. Peel garlic cloves and put into a saucepan with the vinegar. Tie the pickling spice in a small piece of muslin and add to the pan.

Bring to the boil, then reduce the heat and simmer for about 10 minutes. Cool slightly and then strain half the vinegar into a warmed glass jar. Add the eggs then fill up the jar with the remaining vinegar (strained).

Seal with vinegar-proof lids and store in a dry dark place for at least six weeks before using.

Part Two

In the Garden

Planning your Garden – Some Helpful Hints

Enjoy your Garden

Even the smallest garden can provide organic vegetables to keep you healthy, a quota of physical work to keep you fit, and a peaceful environment to nourish the soul.

A little forethought on garden design will reduce your workload, produce larger crops and create a beautiful garden to enjoy.

Decide what you want in your garden. Do you need to keep a play area for the children? If so, you will be better off not planting thorny rose bushes nearby – or any delicate plants that could get damaged by footballs or bikes.

Lawns are very nice to sit on or play on, but they do require a fair amount of

maintenance. If you don't mind mowing the lawn every Saturday afternoon right through the summer months then that's fine but to get the most out of your outside space, it is far more inspiring and practical to be growing herbs, flowers, fruit and vegetables. A short garden path lined with aromatic herbs leading to a seating area takes up no time at all, but is useful and a very peaceful place to relax in.

Get creative and grow herbs in containers or dot them here and there around the garden. Prepare a vegetable plot and if you have enough space, grow some orchard fruit. Fruit trees can be kept very small and trained to grow on a fence or other support if space is limited. These smaller trees are much easier to maintain and to harvest.

And to really set the garden off, plant some sweet-smelling flowers. Roses are always popular, but will need looking after – although a short pruning session once a year should keep them producing blooms year after year. A few bulbs that flower throughout the winter months are worth planting. Flowers in your garden in the coldest months of the year make it all seem worthwhile somehow!

Preparing your vegetable plot isn't difficult. The initial work may be hard but if you are physically challenged, enrol the help of a younger relative or, budget permitting, get a professional in to sort it out for you.

Get the Low-Down on the Dirt!
Ask yourself some practical questions before starting work:

- Is your soil well drained or does it waterlog in the spring or autumn? Can you add gravel or sand to adjust the problem?
- Where is the sunniest spot? And how much shade is available? Some plants need full sun, others prefer partial shade.
- Is the soil tired and/or lacking in fertilisers? Adding green manure or well-rotted farmyard manure will help.
- What depth of soil have you available before hitting hardcore? A very shallow topsoil layer will not be sufficient for root crops.

With these points in mind, choose the best spot in your garden and set to work. Mark off the plot using lines of string attached to wooden stakes. (Tent pegs will do – anything to give you a straight line to work with.) Of course you could decide on a circular vegetable plot, but in practical terms, a square or rectangle will give you more space to grow your veggies.

Using a sharp spade, turn over the earth, working along each guideline of string. Remove all perennial weeds and large stones or any inorganic debris as you go. Don't try to do too much at a time. If you only dig over one length, it's a start.

There's no point in over-doing it and suffering with back pain for the following two weeks!

When the plot is dug, it is a good idea to go over it again – yes, I realise that may sound unnecessary, but the soil will break up nicely and it will give you a chance to remove any weeds not spotted in round one!

Also, you can dig in some manure if required at this stage. Spread it over the ground first, then dig in well.

Test your soil for acidity. If you have a high acid content, you will find brassicas and cabbages etc. won't crop so well. Add a little lime to neutralise the acid if needed.

Your vegetable plot will be where you'll grow all your annual crops. If you have enough space in the garden, prepare a permanent patch as well. Dig over in the same way as you did with the vegetable plot.

Permanent Patch

Fruit bushes, asparagus and many herbs never need moving. Choose your spot well. On a slight incline, fruit bushes may benefit from water drainage by placing at the bottom of the slope but check sunny spots first and follow manufacturers' instructions when you buy new trees and plants. Don't waste money by bad positioning.

If you are starting your fruit trees from cuttings, chances are you already know the optimum spot in your garden but don't be afraid to experiment. The more cuttings you try out the better, and you can reposition them when they are still young.

Permanent patches in your garden need a lot less maintenance but neglect at your peril! Blackcurrant bushes will not provide a heavy crop if their stems are knee deep in weeds! Keep earth clear and well watered around fruit bushes.

Asparagus is a good permanent crop to grow. It needs three years before you can even pick it. But don't be put off. Once established, asparagus will crop year after year, and the plants get bigger and bigger. Indigenous to coastal areas, asparagus loves seaweed, salt and sand and benefits greatly from a comfrey feed now and then (see p. 62). Cut down the asparagus ferns in autumn and layer on as much suitable fertiliser as possible. Build the bed higher every year to ensure the asparagus crowns are deep enough. Asparagus crowns are the roots of the plant and resemble giant spiders.

Herbs are decorative, aromatic and practical plants to have in your garden. Start with two or three favourites and build up your herb garden slowly. Choose those you like to use in the kitchen. Some herbs, such as basil, need to be

planted every year. Basil can be tucked in with the tomato plants in your main vegetable garden and doesn't require its own permanent patch. Other herbs need their own space and will grow into it year after year, developing into usable flowering shrubs.

Pure Pleasure

Your garden can be a place of exercise, good health and total peace! Many people are put off by the 'gardening' word. They imagine it's all digging and weeding. Well, there is some digging and weeding but the rewards outweigh the work.

Don't let your garden become a chore. Use labour-saving gadgets and ideas. Experiment with exotic plants. Avoid chemicals in your natural space – keep organic. Feed the slugs with beer and feed your plants with comfrey. Listen to what gardeners have to say. Some advice may be usable in your garden!

Sprinkle flowers around. Choose easy-to-grow flowers and place them here and there in your vegetable garden. Not only does this provide visual pleasure, it encourages bees and other useful creatures to visit your garden. The scent of flowers while you pull the weeds is intoxicating! Try growing 'statice' – a flower that grows as a ready-made dried flower. The tiny clusters of blooms are like tissue paper and very colourful. Pick them soon after flowering to decorate your home. Place in vases (without water) and create a stunning flower arrangement. Keep them dry and, if possible, dust free.

Finally, provide seating! Have a garden chair, a wooden bench or a fallen log in your garden and use it! After ten minutes digging or pottering, relax and look at your achievements. Sit on your seat and shell peas you've just picked or simply enjoy the moment.

Reduce the Workload!
Raised beds mean less work. The principle of raised beds is to preserve the quality of the soil by not walking on it. Prepare your beds to a metre wide with access both sides.

Once dug, very little maintenance is required. Simple weeding and hoeing will suffice. Using the raised bed method, plants can be set closer together, producing a higher yield from a smaller space.

Add fertiliser as a top dressing in the autumn and dig into the soil in the spring. The beds will slowly get higher, giving a good depth for root crops later on, while storing nutrients for your precious plants.

Pick'n'mix!

To get over rotation difficulties in a small garden, mix up all your crops. Fewer minerals will be extracted by your plants pro rata and some plants will help deter pests belonging to other species. Onions protect carrots from carrot fly, for example, and carrots protect onions from onion fly!

Not all plants like to be together. Here is a list of plants that are good together – or not.

plant	good companions	bad companions
asparagus	tomatoes, parsley, basil	potatoes
beans	carrots, cabbage, cucumber	leeks, chives, onions, garlic
beetroot	onions, chives	runner beans, lettuce, cabbage
broccoli	celery, sage, rosemary	tomatoes, strawberries
carrots	leeks, peas, lettuce, tomatoes	parsnips, chives, radish
celery	beans, leeks, cabbage, tomatoes	parsnips, potatoes
corn	cucumber, parsnips, potatoes	none
cucumber	peas, beans, celery, carrots	potatoes, cauliflower
lettuce	carrots, cabbage, onions	beans, parsnips, beetroot
nasturtium	cauliflower, cucumber, cabbage	broccoli, potatoes, fruit trees
onions	carrots, beetroot, lettuce, cabbage	beans, peas, parsnips, leeks
potato	beans, cabbage, corn	squash, tomatoes, raspberries
peas	beans, carrots, corn, cucumber	garlic, onions
tomato	asparagus, beans, basil	beetroot, broccoli, carrots, onions, parsnips

Companion planting shows good results in tests and experiments and especially on site!

Traditional ideas of planting an 'onion patch' or a 'carrot bed' etc. are proving to encourage problems with pests and plant viruses. When the cabbage white butterfly attacks, it can destroy all your brassica crops in one go. Plant a cabbage or broccoli plant here and there around the vegetable garden and the butterfly

will have a lot more trouble – and you will be able to pick off the offending caterpillars at leisure.

Free Gardening Products

There are many items laying about the house that can be recycled and used in the garden or the potting shed. Here are just a few ideas. Before you throw anything away, give it a second chance!

Comfrey Feed

If you have comfrey growing in the garden, harvest as many leaves as you can, put into a large barrel, or any other suitable container, with nettles. Weigh down with a large stone and cover for a few weeks. Drain off the resulting liquid and dilute with water to make a useful tonic to feed your vegetables with. This can be done a few times a year as and when the comfrey leaves are available. The comfrey tonic helps to release nutrients in the soil for the crops to absorb.

Food Waste

If you can, always compost food waste. Don't put meat products on to a compost heap because you will attract vermin to the garden but all vegetable peelings are perfect for composting. Composting is becoming an art form these days, with many different compost tumblers and barrels available from garden centres and online. But a simple compost heap can be made if you have the space with just a few slats of wood and a little work. Make a box shape with slats of wood and strong corner pillars – maybe old fence posts. Leave a removable slat or two at the bottom of the heap so you can dig the compost out later.

The secret to good compost is keeping the heap fairly warm so, if you can cover it with a dustbin lid, a piece of corrugated iron or old carpets, so much the better. Turn the contents over from time to time to encourage the rotting process. After a year the bottom of your heap will be ready to dig out and you can use to pot your baby plants or, if you sieve it through a fairly fine garden sieve, you may even be able to use it for seeds.

Hedge Clippings and Lawn Cuttings

Rather than putting all your waste hedge trimmings and lawn cuttings in the recycle bin or straight on the compost heap, munch it up and use it! Beg, borrow or buy, if the quantity justifies the price, an electric garden muncher. These munchers will churn everything (up to about an inch in diameter) into a mulch which is perfect for putting round shrubs, fruit trees or perennial herbs. Mulch helps keep the temperature of the soil warm, and also holds the moisture in during hot dry periods.

If you feel the mulch is too acid for the soil, put on to the compost heap. It will break down much quicker if munched up first! Lawn cuttings can be put directly around your shrubs.

Carpets and Boxes

Keep old bits of carpet, lino and cardboard boxes to cover the ground in the winter. If you live in a fairly cool climate and you have a frost every year, wait until after the frost to cover the soil. The frost helps kill off any nasties that may be lurking. After the frost though, cover the land with old carpets etc. This will kill any weeds present and also kill off any perennial weeds that come up every year. Remove the covers from the soil a week or two before you want to start preparing the ground for the spring crops. Black plastic can also be used instead of cardboard and carpets.

DVDs and CDs

Well, Granny may not have had these available when she was younger but she can certainly make good use of them now! Collect all the old discs that are no good to anyone – out-of-date internet connection discs or DVDs that just won't play any more. String them together with some natural twine to make a bird scarer. I know this sounds mean, but when the local bird population eats all your strawberries before you have even got up in the morning, believe me you will want one of these! Put two posts in the ground and hang the line of discs quite low over your plants. The birds are put off by the shiny surfaces and the movement.

You will probably find one or two extra-brave birds but in general, this will help enormously to keep your fruit crops for yourself. You can also use aluminium bottle tops and shiny foil taken from juice, wine or beer bottles.

Clear Plastic

Keep any clear plastic containers that could be placed upside down over a small plant. Mineral water bottles work well. Cut in half widthways and you have two individual mini-cloches to place over your baby plants. Keep

any clear plastic sheets from packaging to cover seed trays or to make small cloches.

Wire Coat Hangers

Make small cloches to protect your young plants in the early spring. Pull the wire coat hanger into a square shape and push the hook into the soil until the natural bend in the wire rests on top of the soil. Place another one a short distance away. Put a sheet of clear plastic over the two hangers to form a tunnel. Use a log or heavy stone to hold the plastic down on either side. These small cloches are good to help keep your baby plants warm in an unheated greenhouse.

Glass Jars

Glass jars with sealable lids are perfect for storing seeds, peas or beans that you will be planting later in the year. And the mice don't have a chance of getting into them! Make sure the jar is perfectly clean and dry. Put it upside down into a warm oven for a few minutes, to dry thoroughly. Use dark jars if possible or you can make clear ones dark by painting the outside or wrapping paper around and tying it in place with string or sticking it down with glue or adhesive tape. Label the jars so you know which seeds are which, especially if you collect your own seeds. It's practically impossible to tell the difference between a gourd and a courgette seed!

Paint Trays

Roller painting trays make great seed trays but any shallow plastic dish will work well for starting off seeds. Punch a few holes in the bottom of the tray for drainage – the soil should never become waterlogged – and add a little fine gravel before filling with your seed compost. Trays used for seeds should be no deeper than 6in (15cm).

Yoghurt Pots

Yoghurt or dessert pots are good for small plants and can be used for individual seed planting. Make sure they are washed and dried well before you store them or they will grow mould. Punch a hole or two carefully in the bottom of each pot before adding a little gravel and filling with seed compost.

Ice-Lolly Sticks

Yes, even wooden ice-lolly sticks have their uses. Wash them first and dry thoroughly. They make great markers. When you are starting off all your seeds in trays and pots in the greenhouse or conservatory early in the year, you really do need to make a note of what has been planted – and where. Wooden lolly sticks can be written on with a pencil, marker or ballpoint pen.

Look out for other things you can use in the garden or potting shed, before you throw them away:

- old kitchen spoons and forks for transplanting small plants in the green-house;
- leaky buckets are useful for harvesting carrots and potatoes;
- light wooden fruit boxes for transporting harvested salad or carrying pots around.

Growing and Storing Everyday Vegetables and Fruit

There are scores of vegetables and fruits we can grow these days in the home garden. With the number of hybrid varieties available to choose from, it's almost impossible to decide. The best first step is to grow what you and your family like to eat. There is no point in growing lines and lines of beetroot if no one in the family likes to eat it!

The vegetables and fruits listed below are all foods which our parents and parents' parents would have grown, or at least cooked and eaten. Start your family recipes off in the garden and produce organic vegetables for even tastier meals.

Vegetables

Broad Beans

Many gardeners prefer to grow their
broad beans through the winter months;
although they can be affected by wind, it
is often easier to deal with supports for the
plants than to try to get rid of blackfly which inevitably
attack the spring-grown plants. Broad beans are gener-
ally a fairly hardy plant and will grow in most soil types. When you buy the
seed, check to make sure you have the right variety for your region and season.
Some hybrid varieties will be good to grow in the spring, while others will be
better suited to winter growing. Always make sure the ground is well drained,
especially for the winter-grown types.

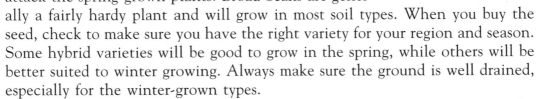

Broad beans don't particularly like an acid soil so, if yours is on the acid side,
add a little lime earlier in the year before planting.

Positioning and Planting

Many varieties grow tall, and will benefit from stakes to support them, especially
during the winter. Avoid windy spots if possible. Before planting the seed, position
the stakes at regular intervals and push into the ground until they are firm. Tie
the plants to the stakes as they grow.

Broad beans do like sun and a strong sunny position is best for them. However,
they have been known to crop well next to a hedge or fence and in partial
shade. Try a few in different places in the garden to see what works best for
you.

Broad bean seed is normally planted directly outside, but if you want to get an
early start to a spring sowing, you could try starting them off in individual pots
earlier in the year. Biodegradable pots are the best pots to use as you can plant
the whole thing in the ground at a later date to avoid damage to the roots of the
plant. Broad beans crop well when started off like this and it's worth giving it a
go if you have access to some biodegradable pots.

Plant out, allowing plenty of space between the plants. Once you have started
off your early plants, sow a short line every couple of weeks to ensure a meal or
two right through the summer.

Care

As mentioned above, blackfly love broad beans. Watch out for an attack. If you do see some, pinch off the tops of the affected plants, and they should be fine. Some growers swear by taking the top off every plant anyway. You should wait until the plant is in full flower before doing so. These plant tops are edible – as long as they aren't housing the dreaded bugs.

Don't let the plants dry out. Water regularly and keep them free of weeds. Hoe gently around the base of the stem every now and then, being careful not to damage the plant.

The whole pod can be eaten when young, but for a full crop, wait until each pod has about four or five large beans. You can tell by the shape of the swellings in the pod!

When the plants have finished producing beans, cut them down to the ground. Put them on the compost heap unless there are any diseased plants, which you should burn. Dig the healthy plant roots back into the ground. All beans and peas help to fix nitrogen into the soil.

Excess

If you have too many broad beans to eat, they can be stored very successfully or made into freezer meals. Dried beans will keep indefinitely and are good to add to soups and stews during the winter months. Let the pods dry completely on the plant until they start to shrivel. Collect the beans and store in a glass jar. Label and keep in a cool dark place.

If the weather is very wet, harvest the beans and dry them off in a very slow oven for a couple of hours. Make sure they are very dry before storing.

To freeze them, shell and lay on trays. Freeze quickly, put into suitable containers and label. Beans can also be canned or bottled if you have the equipment to do so.

Cabbages

Cabbages can be grown all year round, as long as you buy the right variety. There are also different types you could try, like white cabbage, red cabbage and a luxurious savoy! In fact there are hundreds of different types of cabbage and they come in all shapes, colours and sizes.

If you live in a hot climate, you may find that cabbages grown through the summer months may bolt

– run to seed – making them inedible. Grow those varieties which mature before the hot summer sets in and try a couple of different varieties for a change. White cabbage is the main ingredient of coleslaw and can be eaten raw. Green cabbages are usually best eaten cooked.

Positioning and Planting

Cabbages are heavy feeders and will benefit from a fairly rich soil. Dig in some compost or well-rotted manure early in the year. Cabbages belong to the brassica family and none of this family will crop well in acidic soil. Lime the ground before sowing your cabbages if necessary.

They will need a light airy spot in the garden but not full sun. Double check on your seed packet before sowing for individual growing instructions.

Buy small plants ready for direct planting in your vegetable patch or start from seed. You will need to sow seed early in the year in a warm place, a greenhouse or conservatory preferably. Sow the seed in warm, seed compost and keep warm and moist until the cabbages are ready to plant out. They should have at least four true leaves (not counting the first two) before planting out. They will be around 2–4in (5–10cm) tall. Again double-check your seed packet for variety and regional variations.

Allow about 2ft (60cm) between plants when planting in the garden. This will seem a lot when your plants are tiny, but they soon grow, and will need plenty of space to fully mature.

Care

Never let your cabbage plants dry out. Cabbages are 90 per cent water and will suffer if they aren't watered regularly. Use an organic feed every few weeks to encourage the plants to grow well. Try the natural comfrey feed you can make yourself as described on p. 62.

If the weather turns extra cold or windy during the early part of the growing season, protect the plants with a cloche that you can remove later.

The cabbage white butterfly is the one enemy you should watch out for. It's wonderful to see butterflies in our gardens but if you spot a white, sometimes yellowish, plain-looking butterfly lurking around your cabbage patch, make sure they don't lay their eggs, or if they do, remove the leaves and burn immediately. The eggs will be laid on the underside of the leaves. And as soon as those caterpillars hatch, your cabbage patch will almost disappear overnight. They are the hungriest caterpillars in the world! Don't let them take over. If you miss them at the egg stage, you have to be brave and remove them manually, or you will lose your cabbages. If you keep a few laying hens, feed the caterpillars to them!

Harvest your cabbages when they are fully grown.

Excess

Cabbages are high in water content and they don't freeze well, although you can try with a harder variety – slice and blanch in boiling water for a minute or two, then cool completely and freeze in suitable containers.

Cabbages will keep for a few weeks if kept in a cool, dry place, although they will be subject to mice attacks. Hanging in a net from the ceiling helps prevent mice finding them.

The best way to store cabbage for any length of time is by making sauerkraut. Cabbage should be sliced, mixed with salt and weighed down to ferment for a few weeks. It is then kept in sealed jars until required. The fermented cabbage can be used to make soups and be added to stews during the winter months.

Carrots

Carrots are a great source of vitamin A and have been eaten for hundreds of years. They aren't all orange either. Carrots come in all sorts of colours including yellow, purple and red. If you have a good depth of soil in the veggie patch, choose a long carrot but if your soil tends to be rather shallow before hitting coarse stone, grow a shorter, fatter type.

Because carrots are a root vegetable they like a nice clean deep soil if possible. Dig deep and remove all large stones, non-organic debris and any perennial weeds before planting. Till the soil until very fine and rake over until level. Make sure the ground is well drained. Carrots won't tolerate waterlogged soil.

Positioning and Planting

Carrots like sunlight but will put up with a little shade. Always plant carrots directly outside – root vegetables don't transplant well. They will fork if transplanted, if they manage to grow at all. The best way to grow carrots is to do it in short lines and at regular intervals.

Sow a very short line of carrots – up to a metre in length is good enough

in finely prepared soil. Sow the very fine seed thinly because you will need to thin them out later. Water well and keep an eye on weeds for a few weeks. Carrots are notoriously slow to germinate. As soon as you see the first plants coming up, sow another row of seeds, allowing about 12in (30cm) between rows.

When the carrots are 2–4 inches high, thin them out. Leaving one plant every inch, take out all the others, and discard. This is a hard thing to do at first but you will get used to it! After another couple of weeks, thin again, leaving a couple of inches between plants. This time you may find you are pulling up a few very tiny carrots. Eat them as you go along the row, or throw them into the salad bowl. They are full of goodness.

Tip: when thinning, moisten the soil if it is dry to loosen the roots singularly. This will help avoid pulling out more than you want to. The best time to do this job is in the rain – the rain deters the carrot fly!

Carry on thinning your carrots and sowing a new line every couple of weeks right through the summer. Check on your seed packet for regional advice. When you are leaving about 3 or 4 inches between plants, leave them to grow to maturity – or use as you want.

Care

Keep carrots weed free – because they are so slow to germinate, they can be overtaken with weeds. Familiarise yourself with the look of the carrot plant – it is quite distinct with its feathery foliage. Then you will be able to weed without fear of pulling up the carrots too early.

Always keep carrots well watered, especially during long dry periods in the summer months.

Carrots can be left in the ground until late in the year and many varieties will tolerate an early frost. Read the seed packet to check for frost-resistant varieties.

Excess

Carrots can be stored for many months during the winter. Don't wash them before storing though as they will start to deteriorate immediately. Pull up or fork gently out of the ground. Leave to dry and then store in a barrel of dry sand and keep in a cool, dark place. Make sure the barrel is mouse-proof. If you have sacks available and it's possible to do so, hang carrots in the sacks from the ceiling. This will definitely put off the mice.

Carrots can be bottled or canned if you have the equipment to do this at home. Or they can be sliced and frozen on trays, then stored in suitable

containers in the freezer for many months. Carrots are often bought frozen, ready-mixed with peas, and there's no reason why you can't do this at home. Label before storing.

Courgettes and Marrows

Courgettes were relatively unheard of in the UK before the last decade or two. The vegetable was always allowed to mature fully into a large marrow. The marrow was then peeled and cut into pieces and served as a side vegetable or sliced in half and stuffed. Courgettes are far tastier than fully grown marrows and are more versatile in the kitchen. There are many different varieties. Grow a couple of plants that produce round courgettes, or maybe yellow types.

When courgettes get going, you will probably find you can't use them fast enough. Be prepared to give some away, as well as eating lots of them!

Positioning and Planting

Courgette plants are pretty hardy when they get going, and you may even find that they come up on their own in the compost heap! They benefit from a fairly rich soil, and well-rotted manure dug into the ground during the autumn before planting will encourage a healthy crop.

Make sure the site is well drained. Some growers prefer to grow all squash plants (pumpkins, cucumbers, gourds and courgettes) on a mound, to allow for draining. Courgettes prefer a sunny spot but will tolerate partial shade.

Start the plants early in a greenhouse or warm part of the house and keep warm and moist until all danger of frost has passed. Sow two seeds per pot and later, when they have both germinated and have a couple of true leaves, remove the weaker plant. Use biodegradable pots if you can, to avoid damaging the roots when you transplant them into the garden. Don't plant outside until they have at least three or four true leaves (not counting the first two). Soak the plant pot thoroughly with water before removing the plant for transplanting. Plant out in the garden allowing about a metre between plants. Check on your seed packets for advice on your particular variety.

It may seem that you have to allow an awfully big area for such tiny plants but they will grow into the space very quickly.

Care

Courgettes should be kept weed free until the plants become established. The foliage will prevent weeds from growing once the courgette plants are bigger. Keep them well watered all the time but never allow the ground to become waterlogged. When they are small, protect them against slugs and snails. Broken eggshells laid thickly in a circle around the plants will deter slugs and snails.

As soon as the first courgettes appear and are a few inches long or a couple of inches in diameter if growing round ones, cut them and eat! Use a sharp knife and cut just above the stem. And don't worry about using them when they are so small; the plants will be encouraged to produce even more.

The courgette plant is said to be one of the easiest plants for the home gardener to grow, even for the beginner.

You can also plant courgette seed later on in the summer directly outside and with a mild autumn you will be able to pick courgettes until very late in the year.

Excess

You are almost definitely going to have excess produce if you have planted more than a few plants. They can be frozen but won't keep their texture well. Slice them and freeze quickly on trays, then put into suitable freezer containers and label before freezing. Another way of freezing is to make a ratatouille with tomatoes and onions and freeze the whole dish – again freeze as quickly as possible and store in suitable freezer containers. Label.

Courgettes can also be pickled, and are often included in many mustard and everyday pickle recipes.

Lettuces

In Granny's day, there probably would have been only a couple of types of lettuce seed available to grow at home. Cos and a basic cabbage shape were the norm. Now, however, we are really spoiled for choice. Grow a number of different varieties and bring the salad bowl to life all through the summer. There are curly leaved Italian varieties, cut and come again types that you can keep cutting and they carry on growing. And then there are all the little gems, cos and even iceberg lettuces.

Whatever you decide to plant, only plant a few of each at a time. It's always better to sow a few seeds every few weeks than lots at once, unless you are feeding plenty of rabbits or tortoises.

Positioning and Planting

Lettuce seeds can be planted in a greenhouse or other warm place early in the year to get them going for spring salads. The seed is very small and should be sown sparingly. Lettuces tend to germinate fairly well and you will have hundreds if you plant too many seeds!

In a seed tray of compost, sow a few very short lines or plant in pots. Label each line with the type you have planted. Keep the soil moist, warm and weed free. When the plants have come up and are a couple of inches tall, carefully re-plant into another tray if the weather isn't warm enough for planting out yet. Allow a few inches for growing space around each plant. Trays in the greenhouse are perfect for starting off early lettuces.

Always be economical with sowing seed. It's much better to plant a few seeds every 2–4 weeks or so than plant them all at the same time.

When all danger of frost has passed, plant the lettuces out in the garden. This is best done on a dull or rainy day and preferably later on in the day so that the hot afternoon sun doesn't dry the plants out too much. Choose a partially shady spot. Although lettuces like warm weather they don't like too much direct sunlight. The plants 'bolt' – run to seed – very quickly in the hot sun and become inedible.

Lettuces can also be started off under cloches or polytunnels, or directly in the garden when the weather is warm enough.

Winter lettuce can be grown in a greenhouse or warm room and is a great taste of summer in the middle of the winter months.

Care

Keep lettuces watered all the time and weed free. The worst enemies of lettuce are slugs and snails. They really have no scruples at all and will be delighted with the gift of fresh young lettuces. Right from the start, when you are germinating the plants in the greenhouse, be vigilant. Don't let the slugs attack. Use organic means to get rid of them or creep into the greenhouse at night with a torch and catch the little devils. Feed them to the chickens if you have any.

Apart from slugs, just keep the lettuces well watered and steal a few leaves from time to time if you want to – there are no hard and fast rules about having to let the plants fully mature before consuming!

Excess

Lettuces are so high in water content that they really don't store well. A crisp lettuce may keep for up to a couple of weeks in the salad compartment of the fridge, but generally, lettuces should be eaten fresh. This is another reason why it's a good idea to sow a few seeds every few weeks, right through from spring to late summer.

Onions

No chef would ever be without onions in the kitchen and luckily onions are fairly easy to grow in the kitchen garden. Shallots can be grown for a special onion treat and they will grow readily in a moderate climate, as will ordinary everyday onions, everlasting onions and spring onions. Try a few different sorts. Growing everlasting onions in your garden means you will always have a few onions available for the kitchen because they are ready to eat between the last winter stored ones and the new season crop.

Positioning and Planting

Onions like a sunny position and a well-drained soil. They also like to grow in fairly firm ground, so dig over the plot a month or so before planting to let it settle. Remove any large stones, perennial weeds and non-organic debris. And dig in some well-rotted manure or compost.

Onions can be planted from seed, but they can be very slow and temperamental to germinate. The best way to get your onion patch started is to buy onion 'sets': small onions that you plant just below the surface of the ground. Shallots should also be planted from sets.

Spring onions can be planted from seed as they need a shorter growing time and will generally germinate faster than the larger onions.

Plant your onion sets about 6–8 inches apart and use a dibber (a handy hole-making tool) to make the holes rather than a trowel which will loosen more soil than necessary. A stick will do the job just as well if you haven't got a dibber. Plant the tiny onions so that the top is just below surface level and then cover with some loose soil to stop the birds pulling them out. If you have a lot of problems with birds in your garden it may be a good idea to net the onions for a couple of weeks until they get their roots established and start to grow. Use a very fine mesh netting so that the birds don't get their wings tangled.

Care

Onions need watering, especially during the hot summer months but don't be tempted to mulch to keep the moisture in. The onion likes fresh air and will not grow and may rot very quickly if surrounded with a mulch of any sort.

Onions are fairly hardy plants and it is said they will grow happily in a bed of weeds but I have always found they are far happier if given some space, so keep them as weed free as possible.

When the leaves start to go brown they are almost ready to harvest. Fold the leaves down carefully and leave them for a few more days. If the plants should 'bolt' or run to seed, use them straight away as they will not store well.

Pull up the onions on a sunny day and leave to dry on the soil for a few hours. Turn over a few times while drying.

Excess

Onions store well for several months. After they have dried for a few hours in the sun, bring them in and lay in boxes or trays and keep in a cool dark place or plait them in long strings of about 12–18 onions in a plait. Hang them in a suitable place and keep a string in the kitchen just so you can look like a professional chef even if you aren't! Onions that have been carefully stored during the winter will possibly last right through until early spring the following year, although they will start to go soft eventually. Some will probably start to grow again but they won't produce another onion so they should be composted.

Parsnips

Parsnips are a favourite root vegetable, especially in cooler climates. The taste of parsnips improves after the first frost so, in frost-free zones, you can never quite get the best from this delicious root vegetable. However, it is worth growing a few even if you don't live in a cold climate. They are very nutritious and make a great soup or stew addition in the

winter months. They are also used to make wine and beer in rural areas. Parsnips are often given to babies to soothe them and, because of their sweet taste, are used in making cakes.

There are a few different types; some are longer and thinner and others shorter and fatter. Choose which one suits your particular depth of soil and growing region.

Positioning and Planting

Dig over the ground to a good depth and remove any large stones and non-organic debris. Don't add manure to the soil because, as with most root crops, they will fork in a very rich soil. Pull up any perennial weeds and make the ground as clean as you can. They like a sunny position, but as parsnips are a long-growing vegetable, they do take up a space in the garden for the best part of a year, so choose the position well.

They should always be planted directly in the ground, and should not be transplanted. Plant the seed fairly thickly as parsnips tend to be temperamental about germination. Once they get going they will be fine though, so don't be put off. Water the lines of seed after planting very carefully: the seed is very light and can be easily washed away.

Care

When the plants are a few inches tall, thin them to allow a few inches between each plant. Double-check your seed packet for advice on your particular variety. Keep weed free and watered throughout the summer months. Parsnips are fairly hardy plants and don't normally suffer with disease, virus or even pest attacks. A good hardy all-round garden vegetable to grow!

The young leaves can be eaten in salads.

Excess

Parsnips can be left in the ground right through the winter but if you are expecting a few inches of snow or a very hard frost, dig up those required beforehand as it's almost impossible to remove roots from frozen solid ground.

They can be stored in barrels or sacks of sand in a cool, dark place for many months, just like carrots. Keep away from mice, though.

Parsnips will freeze well. Prepare by scrubbing well, or peeling if preferred, although if they have been grown organically, it's best to retain the peel if you can. Cut into fairly thick slices and spread on to a freezing tray. Freeze quickly, pour into a suitable container and label before placing in the freezer. Or prepare a soup or stew with parsnips and freeze the whole meal.

And of course, parsnip wine is always worth having a go at if you have the time, space and equipment.

Peas

One of my earliest kitchen memories is of shelling peas with my grandmother. Children love this job. Every pod contains one pea that has to be sampled, so you get the kids to eat fresh raw vegetables as well as having fun and helping in the kitchen at the same time.

Along with the regular shelling peas, there are mangetout peas available nowadays. They will grow easily in your vegetable plot and can be eaten as soon as they are an inch or two in length. In fact the smaller you eat them, the sweeter they are.

And you could try growing the larger marrowfat peas, which are perfect for making 'mushy peas'. Grow as many as you have space for – they won't go to waste and can be stored for using in the winter, if necessary.

Positioning and Planting

Peas can be planted directly outside very early in the year. Try to prepare the ground as soon as it is workable, digging over and removing any non-organic debris and large stones. Rake over gently, and cover the ground until it is ready for planting. Check on the growing instructions for your particular variety for the best time to plant but you can usually plant peas as early as February or March, depending on the weather conditions.

They won't thrive in waterlogged soil so the site should be well drained. And before planting the peas, you will need some sort of support system in place. Peas like to climb and they curl tendrils around anything in their path, so give them a good support to cling to.

Pea sticks placed firmly in the ground at very close intervals work well. You could use prunings from fruit trees, as long as the sticks have a branch or two for the plants to cling to. Or make a 'fence' using chicken or pig wire or a wooden trellis. Make sure it is firm enough so it won't get blown down in the wind. Never add nitrogen to the soil where you are growing peas. Pea plants 'catch' nitrogen from the air and set it into the ground via their root system.

They will grow in nitrogen-rich soil but will produce more foliage than peas.

They like a bright and airy spot, but as they are a cool climate vegetable, they don't need full sun to grow well.

When your support system is firmly in place, dig a shallow trench along its length and plant your peas allowing an inch or two between each one. Water and protect from birds – and mice.

Care

Don't mulch peas, thinking you should keep the ground warm for them. The stems will rot and the plant will die. They also don't need too much watering and will not thrive in waterlogged ground. Make sure the drainage is good.

In favourable conditions you can almost watch the plants grow. Their strong tendrils will wrap around anything in their path, so don't stand still for too long next to your pea plants!

As soon as the plants start to flower they will be producing pea pods. Keep a careful eye on them, especially if growing a 'mangetout' variety where you eat the whole pod. If they grow too large, the pod will be too stringy to eat. These whole pod types can be eaten raw or stir fried.

Larger peas should be left until the pods are a few inches long; again this does depend on the type you are growing so check on your seed packets for recommended harvesting times.

Excess

Peas are probably the most versatile vegetable when it comes to storing. They can be frozen: freeze quickly in trays then put into suitable containers and label before placing in the freezer. They can be bottled or canned if you have the necessary equipment at home or they can be dried. Dried peas were taken on long sea voyages in olden times and stored very well for many months.

Dry off in the sun or use a home dryer or dry them in the oven. First, shell the peas, blanch for a few minutes in boiling water then drain and leave to cool completely. To dry in the oven, lay out on trays and place in a cool oven for a few hours. Leave the oven door open. Turn the tray every half an hour or so.

Don't stop and start this process as any moisture left in the peas will create a mould and your crop will be spoiled.

When thoroughly dried, store in sealed jars and use during the winter months to make soups and stews.

Potatoes

The humble spud is probably the most regal of all vegetables to grow – a good standby in times of old when money was short and vegetables were not so available. There have always been potatoes grown in the western world – for many centuries anyway. They are so versatile, they can be served every day of the week in a totally different way and there are also many different types that can be grown in a home garden in a moderate climate. You could choose a softer flesh if you serve more mashed potatoes, or a firmer variety for roast potatoes. Grow a couple of different types so you always have the choice.

Positioning and Planting

Planting potatoes isn't just a question of throwing the seed around – oh if only! The initial preparation to get a healthy potato crop takes a fair bit of manual work to prepare the soil although there are other ways of growing. You could try a potato barrel or a raised bed system although, all being well, the traditional way will tend to produce a larger crop.

Always buy seed potatoes to start with. It's true you can grow successful plants from potato peelings but it is unlikely the plants will crop so well. Your seed potatoes should be no larger than a chicken's egg.

Put the seed potatoes in a tray in a dark place for a couple of weeks and allow them to 'sprout'. Keep them out of the light. When they are sprouted they are ready to plant.

While you are waiting for this to happen, prepare the beds. Choose a sunny spot if you can, not too close to where you will be growing tomatoes. They are of the same family and will be more likely to get 'blight' if too close together.

Dig over the ground and remove large stones, non-organic debris and perennial weeds. You can plant potatoes in unworked land and the ground the following year will be easier to dig. However, you will get a vastly reduced crop.

Dig trenches about 6–8in (15–20cm) deep and, if you have any, lay comfrey leaves along the bottom of the trench. The comfrey helps release nutrients from the soil and will encourage more potato tubers from each plant. If not, don't worry! You don't need to put anything in the ground as long as it is fairly well prepared and perennial weeds and roots are removed beforehand. Allow about 2ft (60cm) between rows.

Lay your potato seed in the trenches, allowing about 12in (30cm) between each. Cover the seed with the earth dug out of the trenches and fill. Rake over and water well. Keep weeded and watered and in two or three weeks you will see small bushy plants appearing along the row.

Care

When the plants are about 6–8in (15–20cm) high, gently rake up the earth from between the rows to create a mound over the potato plants. The earth should just cover them. The whole line should now look like a mound about 6–8in (15–20cm) high. These measurements are approximate! After a couple of weeks you need to do the whole earthing-up process again. Make sure you keep the plants watered and weed free.

Then one more earthing-up 2–3 weeks later will be the final time. After that, leave them to grow on their own, but don't allow the crop to dry out, especially in long hot periods. Potatoes need water to help them swell.

When the plants start producing flowers, the potatoes start to grow. A week or two after the flowers have appeared you can gently scrape away the earth in the mound around the plants (don't use a tool for this, you hands are better and will not damage the roots) and pick a few baby potatoes as a treat. You deserve it after all that work!

Let your potato foliage die back before harvesting the main crop. Use as required though and remember there are no hard and fast rules about waiting for all the plants to grow before harvesting all the potatoes. Dig up the plants as you need them, and store the rest. Use a fork to dig them up, allowing a large area around each plant to avoid damaging the potatoes.

Blight can affect potato plants and if you find the disease, which generally looks like a rotting of the stem and leaves, cut down the plant and burn it. The potatoes in the ground should be fine and will even continue to grow for a week or more.

Excess

If you haven't used all your potatoes by autumn time, harvest them or the wet weather will start to rot them. Choose a nice, dry day, and dig up all the plants gently, being careful not to damage the potatoes underneath. Leave to dry out on top of the ground for a few hours, then turn them.

Bring them indoors and store in trays or cardboard boxes in single layers if you have the space. They will keep for many months if kept dry, damp free and out of frost. As with all stored vegetables, keep a lookout for mice. They will home

in on any food products during the cold winter months, especially those vegetables high in water content.

Runner Beans

Runner beans are one of the tastiest beans available and will grow well in moderate climates. They don't like long, hot and dry summers. But they will grow if kept watered and looked after properly. Runner beans do become stringy with age and are best picked fairly young. However, they will still need 'topping and tailing' – the ends cut off, and the string removed from each side. They are not as easy as other green beans – to grow or prepare – but are well worth the effort as they are by far the most delicious!

Positioning and Planting

Dig over the ground and clean well. Beans are best grown in the same patch as peas. They like a light airy position and some sun, but not particularly full sun. Runner beans climb and will need a structure to support them. You can be adaptable with the structure. Many gardeners favour a 'teepee' design. Place long bamboo – or other – canes in a circle firmly in the ground. Bring the tops of the canes together and tie with garden twine. Make sure the structure is firm and will not blow down in the wind. The whole structure can be as much as 8ft (2½metres) high.

Then, with a natural twine, run lines around the bamboo sticks at regular intervals – probably about every 12in (30cm). Make the lines quite tight and secure to the canes with knots around each one. This process takes a little time to prepare but, once done, your beans will be able to get on with the growing bit without you interfering!

After all danger of frost has passed, plant the beans every couple of inches in a circle around the outside of the teepee, as close to it as possible. Water well. Don't be tempted to soak the beans before planting as they often don't germinate or will rot before germination.

Care

Runner beans have a delicate root structure and the roots are close to the surface, so it's best not to hoe, or if you do, do it very gently. Hand weeding is best if

possible. Keep watered and weed free, during the growing period especially. When the flowers arrive, you may need to 'set' them.

If it rains, you're fine, but if not, fill a hand sprayer with tepid water and spray all the flowers individually to set them to the plant. If this isn't done, the flowers tend to drop before the bean has started to grow and then you don't get any beans, just a very attractive teepee! Spray twice a day if you can in dry weather.

Pick as soon as the beans start to get to about 6in (15cm) long and eat them the same day. Keep picking. When beans start to crop they will very likely grow faster than you can eat them, so keep on picking.

Excess

Runner beans will keep in the salad compartment of the fridge or a cool pantry for a number of days, although they are always crisper if eaten fresh. They can be bottled or canned if you have the processing equipment. Or they will freeze successfully. Frozen beans do change their texture but a few bags of runner beans in the freezer during the winter are definitely worth having. Top and tail and blanch in boiling water for a minute or two. Drain well and cool completely. Then lay on suitable trays and freeze quickly. Put into bags or other containers and label before storing in the freezer.

Tomatoes

There really is nothing like the taste of a home-grown tomato. If you feel you shouldn't bother because by the time yours are ready to eat, the ones in the shops are really cheap, think again. The home-grown tomato surpasses all other tastes!

And as you can choose from so many, the decision making could last for months. Get an early seed catalogue to give you a good head start. There are plum, cherry, regular and beefsteak tomatoes. Then you can choose the colour! Not only can we have red tomatoes, but also yellow, orange or even purple.

I like to grow a few different varieties – it's always nice to have a change.

Positioning and Planting

Tomatoes will grow in fairly poor soil but to get a good crop, dig in some well-rotted manure or compost in the autumn before planting. Choose a sunny spot, out of any wind pockets. The ground should also be well drained. Make sure you don't position tomatoes near your potato crop (see section above on potatoes).

In the spring, dig the ground over and remove all non-organic debris, large stones and perennial weeds.

Start your tomato plants in the greenhouse, conservatory or other light and warm place. Fill trays with seed compost and sow the seeds in short lines. Mark which varieties you are growing if you are growing more than one type. You should start your seed as early as possible. Late February or early March is often a good time, although, if there is any danger of the plants getting cold, wait a little while. Double-check on your seed packets for regional variations.

Keep warm and watered until the plants are 8–12in (20–30cm) high. Then they will need re-potting. Plant in individual pots, and always make sure they are well drained. Put a little fine gravel in the bottom of the pots and half fill with potting compost. Put one plant in each pot, and fill to the top with compost. Firm the plant down, top up with more compost if needed and dunk the whole pot quickly into a bowl of tepid water. Put the pots in a warm sunny spot. If the compost has sunk to a very low level in the pot, top up again.

When all danger of frost has passed, the plants should be put outside, unless you are keeping a few in the greenhouse – in which case they should be re-potted in large pots or special tomato planters.

Before planting outside, get your plants used to the outside world by putting the pots out during the day and bringing them in again at night.

Plant out in the garden allowing about 2ft (60cm) between the plants, although again you should double-check on your seed packet for advice on the particular variety you are growing. Each plant will need a support so place a cane in the ground before planting so as not to damage the roots. After placing your tomato plants outside, water well and, using a natural twine, gently tie the plant to the stake.

Care

It's a good idea to grow a few flowers around your tomato plants because they will attract all the good insects. Nasturtiums work well, as do marigolds. Also, you may want to grow some basil in your tomato patch. Basil is the most compatible herb for tomatoes, in the kitchen anyway!

Make sure you keep the tomatoes well watered and feed them every couple of weeks if you can with an organic feed. They are hungry plants and will benefit from a regular feed. Also, as they grow, tie more lengths of twine around the stems and canes – loosely to allow for growth. If the plants droop they could break and die.

As the plants start to grow they will develop extra little branches between the main stem and larger branches, rather like an extra little 'arm'. Pick these branches out otherwise the plant will produce lots of foliage but few flowers, and therefore fewer tomatoes. Use gardening gloves for this job. Tomato plants stain your skin, and some people are allergic to the plants.

Start picking as soon as your tomatoes ripen and eat as soon as possible – on the way back from the garden if you like!

Excess

Tomatoes will store for a few days or a week in a fridge, but they are best eaten fresh. Or you can freeze them. Put them carefully into boiling water for a few seconds to loosen the skins. Then remove the skins and chop the tomatoes. Cook gently until pureed then cool completely. Pour into suitable containers, label and freeze.

You can also dry tomatoes. With four consecutive days of full sunshine, they can be sun dried. But in the UK at the end of the summer, it's not possible to rely on that kind of weather so oven drying is probably the best bet.

Cut tomatoes in half and sprinkle very lightly with sea salt or very finely chopped basil or other herbs. Put the tomatoes, cut side upwards, on a metal rack and put in a slow oven (gas mark 1, 275F, 140C) for about 6–8 hours. When they are thoroughly dry, remove them from the oven and allow to cool completely. Store in plastic bags or other suitable containers and keep in a dry place out of direct sunlight. If 6–8 hours seems a long time to leave the oven on, make the most of it and put a casserole in to cook slowly, or a rice pudding – or both if the space allows!

Fruit

Apples

If you are lucky enough to already have an apple tree in your garden, cherish it! If it doesn't give many apples, give it some TLC and prune it at the end of the summer to encourage it to produce more fruit next year.

If you haven't got an apple tree, consider planting one. They don't have

to be overpowering and shade the house. Position it well in the garden and it could provide you and your family with pounds and pounds of fresh organic fruit every year, along with a natural shady part to sit in when the sun gets too hot.

Positioning and Planting

Positioning a tree in your garden requires some thought, and care should be taken not to plant too near the house or any building. There are, however, many small hybrid orchard trees you can plant that can be trained against a fence and will take up hardly any space in your garden at all. And they will still produce plenty of fruit. Buy a smaller tree rather than a larger one as it will be easier to plant. Check on the growing instructions for individual types.

Whether large or small, the principle of planting is the same. A large hole should be dug for each tree and well-rotted manure or compost can be mixed with the soil you dig out. Place the tree in the hole and hold steady while you fill in around it with the soil mixture already dug out. Firm down with your heel and water well. Place a stake in the ground if required.

Most trees will need to be planted in the autumn or very early in the spring but growing instructions should be referred to for different types of apple and also regional variations.

NB: is your apple tree self-pollinating? If not, you may have to plant another one nearby to allow for pollination.

Care

Keep watered and weed free, especially in the first year of planting. Once the roots have grown and reached down into the deep soil, you will need to water less, although during hot spells, fruit trees can always benefit from watering, to help produce larger fruits.

Water at least once a day during the first summer season. If you are unable to water for a few days make sure you have mulched around the tree to help keep the moisture in the ground.

When the fruits start to grow, thin them out so that only a few stronger fruits are left to grow on every branch. Keep an eye on the birds. If you have problems with birds in the garden, net the tree or trees using a very fine mesh netting.

Fruit trees should be pruned after the last apple has been picked or a little later in the year. Check the growing and care instructions for your particular tree as all varieties will need different treatment.

If you are growing cider apples, lay a sheet under the tree, send someone up the tree and shake the branches until all the apples are felled!

For dessert apples, a little more delicacy is needed: pick the apples when they are easy to separate from the branch and try not to bruise them as you collect them.

Excess

Apples can be stored for several months if looked after properly. Wrap each apple in paper – tissue paper or newspaper is fine. Store apples in single layers in fruit trays or shallow cardboard boxes. Keep in a dry and cool place until required.

Sliced apples can also be dried, although the process is long and laborious. Peel and slice thinly and dry in a very slow oven for several hours, with the door open, or use a home dryer (a piece of equipment designed to dry fruit and vegetables at home). Store in suitable plastic containers or bags when totally dry and cooled completely.

Apples can be puréed and frozen or made into pies and frozen. They freeze very successfully. Peel, core and slice apples. Simmer in a saucepan over a low heat until mushy and leave to cool completely. Freeze quickly in suitable containers.

Blackberries

Blackberries are the perfect complement to apples. Apple and blackberry pies and crumbles have been enjoyed for generations. If you have the space, grow a few blackberry plants. They are hardy plants and will grow as a hedgerow to save more space. Old-fashioned varieties and the wild 'bramble' will have thorns. If you have children, you may want to grow a thornless variety to avoid accidents. Brambles can be very mean!

Positioning and Planting

Blackberries are very hardy plants and will tolerate almost any conditions. In a mature garden it's almost impossible to stop them coming up on their own, very much like nettles. However, if you are planting one of the newer hybrid types, check on the growing instructions as they will vary in their growing needs.

Although you must be able to grow blackberries from seed, I have never heard of anyone starting their own by this method. Buy or beg from a local grower some healthy new blackberry canes and plant where you want them to stay. They won't appreciate being moved later on.

Many new varieties will be self-supporting but some may require support. Rig up a support system such as chicken wire, pig wire or a trellis. Or you could train them along an existing fence. Use the space you have. The canes should be planted about 5ft apart with 10ft between each row.

Plant in the autumn and, if you can, dig in some well-rotted compost in the summer before planting. Although the blackberry will grow in fairly poor soil, it's always a good idea to give it a boost to start off. Water in well after planting.

Care

You really won't need to do too much with blackberries, especially the older thorny types, although always look at recommended growing advice on your canes when you buy them.

Birds can be a problem, as with all fruit, so net with a fine mesh netting if you need to.

Harvest the blackberries as soon as they are ripe and be careful of the wasps. It's a good idea to wear gloves when picking blackberries, especially with the thorny varieties! But having said that, they are a very soft fruit so they should be picked very carefully.

Rather than picking individual berries, you could cut the whole cluster of berries off with a sharp pair of garden snips but first make sure all the berries are ripe. When you go back inside you can remove the berries from the branch on a kitchen board.

Excess

Blackberries don't store well but you can make apple and blackberry pies for the freezer. And blackberries make good jam. Eat them fresh off the plant for the best flavour and nutritional value but cooked with a little sugar and served with ice cream they are a very special treat!

Pears
There are a number of different pears to grow in the home garden or small orchard, and they will be available in smaller, dwarf varieties to suit an average garden. Choose the best one for your region and buy a fairly small tree if possible. And, of course, choose the one you like to eat the most! Young fruit

trees are usually grafted to a hardy stock plant such as a crab apple when you buy them in a garden centre. Plant the whole tree. It will carry on growing and after a few years you won't even see the join!

Positioning and Planting

Pear trees should be treated in much the same way as apple trees. Position well, especially if the tree is going to grow big. If you have bought a trainable hybrid, plant against a south-facing fence or build a small but solid support system for the tree.

Dig over the ground in the area you will be planting and remove any non-organic debris and perennial weeds. Generally, trees are planted in the autumn, but you may find that a hybrid fruit tree will be perfectly OK to plant in spring. Check on the growing instructions before you buy.

Pears like a sunny position and will thrive if looked after well. Plant in a large hole and mix some well-rotted compost with the soil you have removed. Push the soil back into the hole around the tree and push down firmly with your heel. Place a stake next to the tree if free standing. The stake will protect the young tree from wind damage in the first few years. If you have animals that may damage the bark, wrap a piece of chicken wire around the tree to protect it. Wrap fairly loosely and don't attach it to the tree. After planting, water well.

Care

Pears grow very well against a fence in a fan shape and you will get a good harvest from trees grown like this, especially if they are getting plenty of sunlight and water.

If you are training your trees into a fan shape against a fence or any other small hybrid variety, you will need to prune them every year to encourage more fruit the following year.

Prune in mid to late summer and cut back side branches to within about five leaves or about 6in (15cm). If these remaining branches start producing shoots, cut them off as well, unless they are needed to increase the size of the tree or improve the shape. Use sharp secateurs and always think carefully about each cut to maintain a healthy and fruitful tree.

On larger trees, generally the rule of thumb for pruning is to remove dead wood every year during the autumn to winter months.

Excess

Some pears store better than others. The softer varieties won't keep for long and should be eaten as fresh as possible. Jams and conserves can be made from an excess of fruit. And pears can also be dried, in the same way as apples. Peel, core and cut into thin slices. Dry in a very slow oven until completely dry. Cool thoroughly and store in plastic bags or other suitable containers.

Pears can also be made into pies and crumbles and then frozen. Freeze quickly, pack into suitable containers, label and store in the freezer.

Raspberries

There are many different raspberries available nowadays that can be grown in the home garden. Larger fruits can be grown as well as golden and black raspberries. The regular red raspberry has been a favourite for many generations and can be used to make sauces, desserts and even ice creams. They are supposed to be one of the easiest fruits to grow, so for a beginner in the garden, this is an ideal crop to experiment with.

Positioning and Planting

Raspberries are happy with an acid-type soil and will benefit from a fairly rich mix. Dig in some well-rotted compost or manure the season before you plant your raspberry canes. They like a sunny position, as do most fruits, but they have been known to crop wonderfully behind a shed and in other strange and offbeat places in a garden.

Plant raspberry canes in the autumn for fruit the following year. You can plant them in early spring but they probably won't produce any fruit the first year.

Build a firm support system for your raspberries to protect against wind damage, although you should choose a spot out of the wind if possible.

Push some stakes into the ground to a metre high and fix a strong wire between them at about 2½ft (75cm) from the ground, then another couple of wires across at more or less equal distances.

Dig a trench along the row and plant the raspberry canes about 12–18in (30–45cm) along the row. Fill in the trench and firm the canes in with your heel. Water well.

If you are planting more than one line, leave about 2–3ft (60–90cm) between rows. As soon as you have planted them, using a sharp pair of secateurs, cut each cane down to about 10–12in (25–30cm) high.

Care

In the spring, the canes may have sent up new suckers. You can remove these and re-plant them somewhere else. These suckers should always be removed to ensure the main canes keep energy for producing fruit.

Mulch thickly with a good organic material and feed your plants regularly with an organic plant food.

In the summer, you should find that new canes are growing – not the suckers that you remove, but sturdy canes. Tie these to the support system and cut down the original canes. The new branches are the ones that produce fruit.

Later on in the year when these canes have finished producing fruit, they can be cut down. Because raspberries fruit on new wood, clearing out the old canes helps to keep the row tidy and cropping well.

Keep watered and weed free.

Excess

Raspberries will only keep for a day or maybe two and will deteriorate very quickly. They are a soft fruit like blackberries and can be made successfully into jams, desserts, puddings, pies and even ice creams and sorbets.

Eating them fresh is the most nutritious way of enjoying raspberries and walking round the garden with a handful of freshly picked raspberries is a joy to be experienced.

Strawberries

Strawberries and cream with a light sprinkling of sugar brings back memories of warm summer days and childhood games. The strawberries in the shops are reasonably priced these days but, like so many other fruits and veg, home-grown ones are just the best!

There are different types to choose from – larger fruits are available and different varieties could be tried if you have the space, or stick to an everyday regular strawberry that crops well and is easy to grow.

Positioning and Planting

Buy plants from a reputable garden centre or start your strawberry bed from the baby plants that local growers or neighbours are getting rid of. Strawberries will also crop at different times of the year so it's a good idea to buy a few plants that will crop every couple of months from spring to late summer. Don't be tempted to use wild strawberry plants to get your bed going. It won't work well, and wild strawberries are *very* different from the hybrid varieties we grow at home.

Choose a sunny spot for your strawberry bed but make sure that it isn't on the same ground that has grown tomatoes, potatoes or peppers in the previous few years. Stake off a patch and if possible, surround with large logs or bricks to create a bed that can be filled more and raised a little as years go by.

Strawberries should be moved every three years but the raised bed will be useful for other plants.

The ground should be dug over in the autumn before spring planting and well-rotted manure or compost should be incorporated into the soil. Also remove any perennial weeds and large stones etc. Cover the ground over the winter to avoid further weeds growing and remove the covering a week or two before putting in your plants.

Plant your strawberry plants so that the soil covers the roots completely but not the 'crown' – the centre part – of the plant. Allow about 12in (30cm) between plants and 18in (45cm) between rows. Double-check on the growing instructions for your particular variety though. Water the plants well.

Care

There are many conflicting theories about growing strawberries. Because of the various different types you can grow, check on instructions and go with your instincts. Generally though, plants should be kept weed free and watered, and during hot summer months should be mulched to keep the moisture in the ground.

However, when the fruits start to develop, they are very vulnerable to slug attacks. Remove any mulch that hasn't rotted down, and replace with very dry, clean straw. The straw will deter the slugs and will also allow the strawberries to be out of contact with the damp soil, which can cause them to rot.

Birds can also be a big problem with soft fruits and a fine mesh netting will help save your crop from the birds.

Some growers insist that you should pick off all the flowers in the first year of planting. You won't get any fruit that year but the plants will get stronger for the following year, and will produce more fruit.

Strawberries are not frost resistant. When they start to grow in the early spring months they should be covered with a cloche if there is any likelihood of a frost.

Every year you should remove the new plants that the parent plant sends

out on runners. This will keep the bed clean and tidy and the parent plants will produce more fruit. These baby plants can be used to start another bed. As a new bed should be started every three years, if you have enough space in the garden you can rotate three beds quite successfully, using these baby plants.

Excess

Strawberries will only keep for a few days once picked but can be frozen if done carefully. Pick off any leaves and stalks, freeze on trays quickly and put into suitable containers. Label and store in the freezer. Frozen fruit will not keep its texture though and fresh fruit is far more enjoyable and nutritious.

The best way to keep an excess of strawberries – something I've never managed to achieve! – is to make jam.

Backyard Chickens

Years ago, especially during the war years and after, many households used to keep a few laying hens. Even in the smallest backyard it was considered an acceptable thing to do.

Before you start though, make sure you won't come up against any local regulations preventing you from keeping livestock. Check with your local council offices. When you have a green light, do some research on:

- housing and equipment
- laying hens
- caring for your hens
- costs

Housing and Equipment

Keeping hens in a restricted area is often necessary unless you live in a park or woodland. They will scratch your vegetable plot and eat your new lettuces if allowed to. Most hens don't fly and a 6–8 foot high chicken wire enclosure will be sufficient. The wings can be clipped if you do have flying hens though – a painless process but it should be done by someone who knows what they are doing.

Egg producers say that you should allow a square metre per hen but if you allow them more space you will have happier hens and more egg production!

A coop is necessary and if you have a few DIY skills you should be able to make a reasonable hen house for your birds. A small shed is workable. Make sure they have perches to roost on and nesting boxes to lay their eggs.

If you aren't able to give your hens fresh food and water every day, buy dispensers to do the job for you.

Laying Hens

You will need a local supplier of laying hens. Buying your hens at the point of lay is usually the best way for most new chicken lovers! (The point of lay is the age when a hen starts to lay eggs.)

If you have a rooster, your eggs will be fertilised and the hens are more likely to become broody. They'll sit on whole clutches of eggs and get very tetchy if you try to take them! If you can avoid your hens getting broody, you will have better egg production.

However, if you have children, bringing new chicks into the world is a magical experience. I have spent many Easter Sundays with my children in the hen house cuddling new fluffy chicks!

Caring for your Hens

Hens are originally woodland birds and their feet are specially designed to scratch the surface of the ground and peck at the insects that reside there.

Keeping your hens on a woodland patch is ideal. The next best is grass. They will scratch and spoil the surface eventually unless you have just a few hens on a large area. The best thing to do is change their space every few months to let the earth recover and give them a new spot to unearth the grubs and bugs.

As long as they are on grass or woodland, they will only need a handful of corn thrown to them every day, but if they are unable to scratch as they would in the wild, you'll have to supplement their diet with prepared meals. These should be available at your local farm shop, or livestock supplier. Try to give them some plant food as well, and they will need grit if they live on a sterile or smooth surface.

Give them the lettuces that have run to seed in the garden or the dandelions you aren't using for jam. They eat practically anything! Fruit is always good for birds. Try them with any of these:

- the inside flesh and seeds from melons
- apple cores
- windfall fruits with maggots

They will also be happy with slugs, cabbage white caterpillars and various other bugs you may collect from around the garden.

Cost

It's not easy to do the costings for your egg supply. The equipment, housing and initial cost of your laying hens will certainly mean your eggs are a lot more expensive than the ones you buy in the supermarket, for the first year anyway – maybe even two years. But the experience is certainly worthwhile and the eggs are so much tastier than any you'll buy in a shop!

Part Three

In the Parlour

Needlecraft

Needlecraft is a collection of skills. Any piece of work – or art – performed with a needle is considered to be needlework. There are many different forms, from knitting and crochet through to lacework and embroidery.

Sewing and knitting are probably the two most practical skills you can have. If you can sew a basic seam, you can make clothes and accessories for around the home and repair items rather than having to replace them. If you can knit, then all forms of jumpers, cardigans, scarves and hats can be produced to keep the family snug and warm.

Neither skill requires a college degree or months of expensive night classes. The following pages take you through the basics and, from there, your imagination will be the only thing holding you back!

Sewing

To get used to sewing techniques and the whole idea of doing such a thing, buy yourself a small sewing kit, if you haven't already got one, and find a scrap of material, preferably cotton, to practise on.

To start with, you only need a needle, some thread and a pair of scissors. When you are sure you want to get serious with your new hobby, treat yourself to a sewing basket and fill with the following items:

Scissors, tape measure, a container of pins, another one for needles, a thimble and maybe, if you can get hold of one, a darning mushroom. A pincushion is useful and a safety pin or two, as well as tailor's chalk and a seam ripper.

Buy a few different reels of thread in different colours – black and white are always useful to have available. A razor blade or other sharp blade can be used to rip out seams, although extreme care should be taken when using these kinds of tools. The blade can easily tear the cloth, as well as damage your fingers if you're not very careful. You will also need to have access to an iron and ironing board for pressing seams.

First things first – if your cloth is lightweight cotton, you should use a small-gauge needle and, with a heavier material, use a thicker needle. Try it out and see what feels better. There are no hard-and-fast rules but, if you try to push a very fine needle through a piece of heavy denim, it's likely the needle will break and you could injure yourself. Think about the needle matching the cloth before you start. If you just gently push the needle through the cloth and it goes through easily, then that's probably the right tool for the material. If not, try a different combination.

Thread your needle by pushing the thread through the eye by hand or by using a needle threader if you find this too awkward or hard to see. A needle threader is a small metal gadget that is easily pushed through the eye of the needle. The thread is pushed through the threader and then pulled back through the eye, leaving the needle threaded. A needle threader is a handy tool to have, especially if you are tired or the needle is particularly fine.

Step One
When your needle is threaded you are ready to start sewing. Pull about 18in (45cm) of thread through the needle, and cut from the reel so that you have a double thickness of thread.

Making a Start

You can tie a knot to form a secure end but, to get a professional finish to your work, it's best not to get into the habit. Push your needle through the work from back to front and then back through the cloth a small distance away. Now pull the thread through so that there is about an inch or so at the back of your work. Now push your needle up through the same hole – or thereabouts – and back again, to form a double first stitch. Pull thread so that it is firm but not pulled too tight, making sure that you don't pull the end through. Repeat once more and you will have a flat and professional secure start to your sewing.

Running Stitch

Practise some simple stitches to get the feel of the tools and materials. To make a straightforward running stitch, simply push your needle up through the cloth and back through, a small distance away and then up again, trying to keep your stitches in a straight line. Don't pull too tight so that the material puckers. Keep the cloth flat and the stitches firm but not tight. Running stitch is the basic stitch used in smocking, but in that particular type of needlework, the stitches are pulled to produce gathers in the work.

Backstitch

For a solid stitch that won't pull, use a backstitch. Work one running stitch as before then bring the needle up through the cloth a short distance away and then take the needle back down the hole you went down last time. This will fill the gap between the stitches. Now bring the needle up a short distance in front of the last upward movement and then back down to fill the gap again.

Hemming

To form a neat hem for towels, sheets, tea towels, handkerchiefs and serviettes, first you will need to have some pins and preferably an iron. It isn't a hundred per cent necessary to press the cloth beforehand, but it does make it easier to sew.

Fold about 1cm of your cloth along one edge and press with a hot iron – as long as the cloth is cotton or linen. If not, use a cooler iron. Repeat on all the edges. Then fold the edges over once more and press again.

To keep the hem folded in place while you work, either pin or tack. Pins should be fine and lightweight to avoid making holes in the cloth. Tacking is simply making fairly large running stitches and taking care not to let the cloth pucker or pull anywhere. After the hem is finished, this tacking is removed.

Thread your needle with cotton that matches the cloth and begin as described above. Make small backstitches as close to the folded edge as possible, keeping the right side of the work facing you and the wrong side facing down. Work all the way round the hem and then fasten off by sewing a couple of stitches on top of each other before cutting the thread. Whenever you run out of thread, fasten off as neatly as possible then re-thread the needle and begin again. It's important not to have too long a thread when you sew as it can become tangled and will be less easy to work with. The extra time taken to re-thread your needle is time well spent!

Keep the stitches as small and neat as you can.

To create a pretty edge to a serviette, towel, or any other cloth, choose two different colours of silk thread and thread your needle. You may have to separate the strands when you buy silk thread. If so, use 2–4 strands depending on the finish you want. Thread your needle with one colour and sew a running stitch all the way round, taking care to begin carefully and finish in the same way. Try to make all the stitches the same size, as well as the gaps between them, and be very careful the work doesn't gather. Keep your sewing flat and pull gently if it is puckering at all.

Then thread your needle with the other colour and bring your thread up through the same hole as the first stitch, casting on as neatly as possible behind the work. Then thread the needle though the first running stitch from right to left, not through the cloth, just through the stitch. Then thread the needle through the next stitch from right to left and so on until you reach the end of the running stitches.

Step Two

Now, you have mastered the straight stitches used in hemming and decorative edges, as well as tacking and even smocking, it's time to turn our attention to other useful sewing techniques.

Sewing on a Button

What used to be a simple task for every 'housewife' has turned into a nightmare job for most of us. Often we end up throwing a garment away for want of a button! And it really isn't a difficult task to perform . . .

Remove all the old threads where the button has come loose or fallen off. Thread the needle and make a couple of securing stitches in the exact place where the button was before. Now take the needle up through one of the holes in the button and then back through the other hole, or in the case of a four-hole button, the diagonally opposite hole and then push through the cloth. Don't pull too tight. Make a small backstitch at the back of the work and repeat the step until you have sewn through the button at least four times. Then take the needle up through the cloth behind the button but not through it, and wind the thread around the stitches between the button and the cloth. Then push needle through to the back of the cloth and fasten off.

If the button has four holes, take each stitch across diagonally and then stitch the other way. Repeat until you have at least three stitches on each diagonal. Then wind the thread around the stitches behind the button as before. Then fasten off.

Darning a Hole

Darning socks is hardly worth our while these days, with socks being cheaper than the thread we buy to repair them, but other items can be darned and with a little care a garment can be almost as good as new. Darning is almost like weaving, and should be done with a very pointed needle.

Side Note

If you can get hold of a darning 'mushroom' – which is a wooden or sometimes plastic mushroom-shaped tool – you'll find it very useful. The area to be worked on is stretched over the cap of the 'mushroom' and can be held tight underneath it to prevent slipping. It is easier to produce a neat finish if you have one of these. An old-fashioned haberdashery, needlecraft shop or an enthusiastic needlewoman may have one spare. Ask around.

Trim off the frayed edges of the hole to be darned very carefully, making sure you don't pull out any more threads than necessary. Work with the right side of the work facing you and begin at the edge of the hole on the wrong side of the work. If the hole is more or less a perfect square or rectangle, choose a corner to start. Once you have secured the thread, take the thread across the hole, and into the cloth on the other side. Push it through to the back and pull the thread so that it lies across the hole, but don't pull it tight. Now bring the needle up a very small space away, and take the thread across to the other side. Push the needle down through the cloth leaving a very small space. Bring the needle up again a short space away and go across the hole. Continue in this way until there are lines of thread running one way across the hole from top to bottom. Make sure you don't pull the cloth out of shape. The darn needs to blend into the shape of the item. Fasten off, re-thread and begin again as required.

Now, start from the opposite corner and take the thread across the hole the other way (for example vertically instead of horizontally) but this time thread the needle up and down through the lines of thread as if you were weaving. Take the thread down and up again at the opposite side, then return. Keep the lines very close and continue until the hole is completely darned.

Taking up a Hem

Tackle a hem adjustment when you feel comfortable with sewing as it is rather more fiddly than other forms of sewing. Always pin and then tack a hem up before starting to sew. After tacking, remove the pins. Press the tacked hem ready for sewing or, if you prefer, press first. But this can be

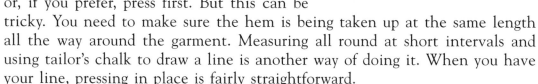

tricky. You need to make sure the hem is being taken up at the same length all the way around the garment. Measuring all round at short intervals and using tailor's chalk to draw a line is another way of doing it. When you have your line, pressing in place is fairly straightforward.

Once you know the exact measurement, fold over the hem and pin at regular intervals. Then either tack the hem or draw a line, press and then pin and tack. The more preparation you do, the better the finished job will be, and also it will be a lot easier to sew. When tacked in place, remove pins as they tend to get in the way.

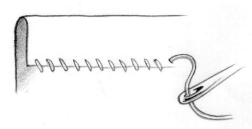

Side Note

Never take up too much material. If the required length needs to be reduced by more than a couple of inches, the hem should be cut first. The cutting must follow the line of the existing hem. Use tailor's chalk for this job. Cut about 1-inch longer for a fine cloth and a little more for a heavier cloth. Then fold the hem over twice to seal in the cut edge and pin and tack.

Thread your needle with matching thread and begin by making a backstitch as described before, into the double thickness of cloth and not going through to the front of the garment. Now, very carefully pick up a thread from the single layer of fabric as close as possible to the folded edge and pass the needle and thread through this thread. Then pass the needle into the folded hem edge and out again a short space away, making sure that you don't take the needle through the front of the garment. Pick up a thread as before and continue in this way until you have completed the hem. Remove the tacking at the end.

Fasten off, re-thread and begin again as needed.

Alterations

Many clothes can be altered to fit although jeans can be particularly difficult. Experiment if you feel you have the time and patience but the many double seams involved are a nightmare to get right!

Simple skirts and plain trousers can be altered to fit without too much trouble, although if you have a sewing machine, you may find it easier to use this to get a professional finish.

Simply unpick the seams and re-sew taking the line of sewing a little further in from the original line. This will make the item smaller. Many clothes will not have much of a seam to let out but it's worth checking before you throw it away!

Waistbands should be carefully unpicked and re-sewn back on to the main part of the skirt after adjusting to fit. Elastic waistbands probably won't need adjusting. A slightly smaller length of elastic is possibly all that will be needed.

When the seam has been unpicked, remove all stray threads, and pin and tack in place before you start sewing. This preparation will ensure a better finish to your work. When the seam has been sewn, remove tacking and press the seam open or flat, depending on how it should lay.

Step Three

Sewing skills can be practised until perfect. They are skills that all of us can perform, even if you believe you never could. Unless you have problems with dexterity in your hands, there is no reason why you couldn't perform the following tasks even if initially they may seem to be for the professional dressmaker.

A sewing machine is a great tool to have. Sewing jean zips in by hand, for example, takes a lot of time and it's an awkward job. However, it's not impossible!

Threading Elastic

A piece of elastic that has broken or simply worn out can make a skirt or a pair of trousers unwearable. Carefully unpick the joining seam on the inside of the waistband, to gain access to the old piece of elastic and remove it. Measure the width of the old elastic and buy a new piece exactly the same size. The length will depend on the size required. Make sure the length of your elastic fits around the waist, comfortably but firmly. Pull to test the best size for you. Then cut the elastic about 2 inches longer than required.

Pin a safety pin to one end, and make sure it is fastened properly. An old-fashioned nappy pin is good for this. They tend to be more secure. However, not all waistbands are large enough to accommodate a nappy pin!

Push the end with the safety pin into the waist band and edge along the length making sure you don't pull the other end of the elastic into the waistband and out of sight. Gather up the cloth a little so this can be done without losing the end.

When the end has come right through and out the other side, place one edge of the elastic on top of the other and backstitch firmly in place. Use a machine if you have one available. Go over the stitching lines in a square shape, securing both ends of the elastic firmly together.

Remove the pin and allow the elastic to gently ease its way into the waistband. Oversew the seam you first un-picked. See 'cushions and covers' for an illustration of oversewing.

Making a Buttonhole

To create a buttonhole you need to have a little patience. It takes longer than you think at first. When you've done a few, it gets easier though! The buttonhole would be normally on the edge of the item and through two layers of fabric. Your needle size and thread should be compatible with the thickness of the cloth.

Cut through the fabric using a sharp, pointed pair of scissors in order to make a straight cut the same diameter as the button you will be wanting to push through. Then make a line of running stitches, or backstitches if the fabric frays a lot, close to the edge of the cut along both sides and across each end. If the fabric is particularly fragile or frays very easily, make the line of running stitches before cutting the cloth.

Re-thread your needle if necessary and make a blanket stitch edge (see below) all along both sides and each end of the hole, taking each stitch just outside of the running stitches so they are hidden.

Blanket/Buttonhole Stitch

Secure the thread on the wrong side of the cloth as neatly as possible and bring the needle up at any point along the line of running stitches, so that the running stitches are between the needle and the cut edge. Then take the needle over the cut edge and back through the cloth next to where you pushed the needle through last time. Now pull the thread firmly but not too tight, and push the needle through the stitch you have made so that the thread sits at the edge of the buttonhole.

Then bring the needle from the wrong side to the right side and repeat all the way round the buttonhole, keeping the stitches as close together as possible. Remember to make the solid edge by passing the thread though every stitch before making the next stitch.

Sewing in a Zip

If you are replacing a broken zip, look carefully at how the zip is sewn into the garment. Different designs call for different methods of inserting zips into clothes. A zip in a pair of jeans may be inserted very differently from a zip in a ball gown – but, then again, it may be exactly the same! You must replace the zip in the same way or the garment won't be wearable.

Remove the old zip using a small sharp-pointed pair of scissors, snipping the stitches carefully so as not to damage the cloth. Pin and tack the new zip in place, exactly as the old one was. Remove the pins once the zip is tacked in place.

Thread your needle with matching thread and follow the line of stitching from before. If, when you remove the thread from the old zip, the stitch line isn't visible, draw it with a piece of chalk so you will know where to stitch. Use a very neat line of backstitches and make sure the thread is pulled firm but not too tight. At the base of the zip, go over the stitch line several times for extra strength. Then remove the tacking stitches.

Appliqué

The art of appliqué is not as hard as it sounds. Appliqué is the application of a picture or design in a contrasting material sewn on to a cloth item. You find babies' blankets with appliqué designs on them, as well as children's clothes and scatter cushions. A silk or satin material is often used but any material will do as long as you can get a needle and thread through it!

Decide on your materials first. Choose a contrast cloth that will suit the garment or other item you are working on. Cut out the shape you want and pin and tack the shape to the item where you want it. Remove the pins so you are left with just the tacking. Using a matching thread, thread your needle. Begin by using two small stitches, on the wrong side of the material, worked on top of each other for strength.

Then bring your needle up through the work close the edge of the new piece of cloth and take it down through the main piece a short distance away from the edge. Bring the needle up again very close to the last stitch. All stitches should be very close together all the way round, and should be the same size and as neat as possible.

Fasten off, re-thread and begin again as required, making sure the first stitch is always very close to the last one.

After practising the stitches shown in Steps One, Two and Three, you will have a basic understanding of the art of sewing. There are many other forms of sewing you can attempt. From making clothes to creating beautiful lacework chair covers, the list is endless. On the following pages, there are a few ideas to further your sewing experience.

Step Four

The following needlecraft skills do require a little patience and plenty of practice to perfect. However, if you enjoy creating beautiful items for your home and family, you will love to explore the needlecrafts that were thought to be a normal part of growing up in every girl's life a couple of generations ago. A young woman was considered highly eligible if she could sew and knit!

Being handy with a needle opens up all sorts of hobbies and pastimes to investigate. You could, for example, try your hand at tapestry, rug-making, lacework, upholstery, dressmaking and smocking. All these crafts require a book to themselves and need special tools and equipment. However, they can all be done at home and take up very little space compared with some hobbies.

Always have a place to keep your work – a basket or clean drawer – to keep it safe from damage. There are often sharp tools involved so your work should always be stored out of the reach of children and pets.

Don't expect to be able to turn out a professionally finished product on your first attempt. Unless you are very talented in this area, it's unlikely the first attempt will be perfect. But one of the nice things about home produce is that it *isn't* perfect. It won't be the same as everyone else's. And you will never find another item exactly the same, however hard you look.

Every item you produce, whether it's a rug, a chair-back cover or a beautiful christening dress, will be unique. Personalise to your heart's content!

When you have mastered the basic stitches in the first three steps, there is no reason why you shouldn't have a little dabble in embroidery. If the word embroidery has you grimacing and thinking of intricate rose designs over linen tablecloths that no one dare use for fear of spoiling, it doesn't have to be like that!

Embroidery

Before starting to sew, decide on your design. There are transfers available that can be ironed on to cloth. You could also try drawing your own design using a fine piece of chalk or a dressmaking pen that won't stain. Special copy paper and a dressmaker's tracing wheel can be used to transfer images on to cloth.

When you have your design ready to embroider, choose your colours and buy the silks needed. Embroidery silk creates a good finish although any thicker thread or very light yarn can be used.

Make sure you have the right sized needle for the job and make a start. Separate the strands of silk if you want a thinner thread and then thread your needle, making sure you don't have too long a thread to work with.

An embroidery ring is a good tool to have as it keeps the material taut while you work and prevents slipping.

The stitch described above in the appliqué section is a basic filling-in stitch and can be used to 'fill' leaves, petals and other designs. Begin by using a very small securing stitch and then bring the needle up on to the drawn line on the edge of the part you want to fill. Take the needle across and down on the other side of the drawn design. Make sure all stitches are very close together but not pulled too tight. The material needs to be kept flat at all times.

There are many other stitches used in embroidery, including the well-known daisy stitch. Practise this until you have the knack of getting the stitches of an equal size. Secure the thread and bring the needle up through the cloth from the wrong side to the right. *Then take the needle back down very close to the point of entrance. Leave a small loop. Now bring the needle up to the right side again through the loop a short way from the original point of insertion. Then take it down again on the outside of the loop so the loop lies flat on the cloth. Go over this small stitch once more by bringing the needle up again at the other end of the small stitch you just created.* Then repeat from * to * until you have a line of daisy chain stitches.

Practical Patterns

Dressmaking patterns can be found in haberdasheries and shops that sell material and needlecraft products, and also in magazines. To reproduce your own pattern use a heavy tissue paper at minimum, although a lightweight brown paper is much more practical, and can be used many times. You can also make notes on the paper without fear of it tearing. Buy a large roll, making sure that the width of paper is wide enough for the widest part of your pattern, or if you can't find anything the right size, you could stick two widths together with paper glue. Make sure the glue is properly dry before you place it on your cloth. Try your hand at the following patterns. Get imaginative and create family heirlooms!

Patchwork Bag

A simple and practical bag can be made from scraps of material. Make sure all the material is the same weight. Thin material doesn't sit well with heavy denim for example. To make a heavy-duty, strong bag – suitable for shopping or even travelling – use a strong cloth. If you have kept the legs of old jeans after they have been cut down for shorts, use them up now!

Cut squares or rectangles to the size you want. The larger the patches, the fewer you need. Work out the size you want your bag and cut out the squares accordingly. A little maths needs to be done here – but it's fairly straightforward. For example, if you want your bag to have a finished measurement of 15in (39cm) wide by 12in (30cm) high and around 4in (10cm) deep, you will need to cut squares or rectangles of cloth to fit these measurements. Make a paper pattern first so you don't make a mistake.

To create a denim patchwork bag with rectangular pieces of denim to the size mentioned, cut the following pieces:

- 27 pieces of denim measuring 6in (15cm) by 4in (10cm)
- 1 piece of denim measuring 34in (88cm) by 5in (13cm)

(If you haven't got a long piece of denim available, use a different piece of cloth but make sure it is around the same weight as the denim.)

If you want to line the bag, cut:

- 1 piece of finer cotton material measuring 32in (92cm) by 16in (42cm)
- 1 piece of finer cotton material measuring 34in (88cm.) by 5in (13cm)

Using a backstitch, or a sewing machine if you have one, sew together the short ends of three rectangles of denim, in a line, sewing half an inch in from the edge. Then repeat until you have nine strips of three pieces sewn together. Press the seams open to get a neater finish. Then stitch together six strips along the long edges, half an inch in from the edge as before. And stitch the other three strips of three in the same way.

Press all the seams open. Now you should have two pieces of cloth, one of 3x3 rectangles and the other 6x3.

The long strip of cloth is the 'gusset' of your bag and provides the depth needed. Allowing a half-inch seam, pin one edge of the long strip along one short edge of the smaller piece of cloth, then take the strip around the corner, along the bottom edge and up the other side. Make sure you pin the right sides together. Tack and then sew with a firm backstitch or use a machine.

Now pin the other long edge of the gusset strip down one edge of the other piece of cloth, matching the end of the gusset strip to the middle of the long edge of the cloth. Make sure you have positioned the right sides together correctly. Pin the bottom edge of the cloth along the strip and up the other side. Tack, then sew firmly in place. Remove all tacking and press the seams open.

Now you have a bag shape. Form the same shape with the lining material and then, folding over raw edges, sew in place close to the edge of your bag on the inside.

To make a strap, cut a long strip of heavy cloth the width and length required and sew in the raw edges. Line with a finer material if required. Backstitch or machine stitch the ends of the strap firmly in place before sewing the lining into the bag. The lining will cover the join.

The bag could be fastened with a strip of Velcro, stitched or stuck in place, or left as it is.

Smocks for Kids

Smocks for cooking and painting and all other messy jobs are a must for under-fives – and you can make one for your child by following a few simple steps.

The easiest way to make a practical smock for your child is to first get out a tape measure. Measure from the shoulder to the knees or length required. Double this measurement and add an inch for hemming.

Measure across the width needed (a little wider than the width of the back of the shoulders), again adding an inch for hemming, and note down these two measurements.

You will need a piece of cloth – washable and lightweight – as big as the two measurements you have taken and allowing a strip that is long enough to use as a belt – an inch or two wide, and long enough to tie around the child and into a bow at the back.

You will also need some binding tape for the neckline – no more than a metre will be needed unless you wish to bind the hem, sides and belt too. Use a contrasting colour to brighten up the smock or a matching colour if preferred.

Cut the rectangle of cloth to the exact measurements.

Cut a straight slit in the cloth exactly in the centre and halfway between the top and bottom of the cut piece, about half the width of their shoulders. Try it over the head to see if it fits; if not, make the slit slightly wider. Make sure it is exactly in the centre though.

Once the hole is big enough, shape slightly by cutting a very small curve in the front, so it's not too tight on the neck when worn.

Hem or backstitch the binding tape with matching thread, or use a machine, all around the neck opening.

Then hem all around the outside edge of the cloth or bind with the binding tape. Make a belt by folding a strip of material in half lengthwise, tucking in the raw edges and sewing along the length with a sturdy backstitch or a machine.

Pop the smock over the child's head and tie around the belt at waist height.

Cushions and Covers

Cushions can be made to enhance your furniture, as large seating areas, or simply to decorate a pretty bedroom. The materials and methods are simple and your imagination could really help you create some beautiful cushions for your home.

Basic Cushion

Decide on the size you want and add about half an inch all around for hemming. Use a simple white cotton for the cushion and either buy a cushion pad or use an anti-allergy filling.

With the right sides together and the wrong side facing you, sew around three sides of the cushion, allowing half an inch all round. Chalk a line if you have trouble sewing in a straight line. Use a machine if you have one to sew the cushions. It's much quicker. Turn the cushion the right way out and place the cushion pad inside or stuff it using the filling material.

Turn in the top edge and oversew the two sides together with very small stitches.

Cushion Covers

Cushion covers are easy to make and should be removable so you will need a zip or piece of Velcro as long as one edge – a short edge will do if the cushion is not a square. You also need the material to be large enough to fit the cushion.

The cover should be cut about an inch and a half larger than the cushion, all around. With right sides together, backstitch or machine sew a straight line round three sides about half an inch from the edge. Turn the right way out and try on the cushion to make sure it fits snugly

but not too tight. If it doesn't fit properly, start again, adjusting as necessary.

Once you have a good fit, insert a zip or stitch Velcro to the open edge, making sure all raw edges have been properly tucked in and sewn in place.

Knitting

Knitting is a relaxing and creative hobby but you need to be comfortable to start. You'll notice that tiny muscles in your hands may ache or you may feel tension in your neck and shoulders at first, but persevere and the muscles used will become stronger and won't ache.

Don't overdo the sessions. It doesn't matter if you only spend fifteen minutes a day on your knitting – this will increase rapidly if you keep at it. Take it slowly and steadily. Your results will be your reward.

Before you begin you will need the right tools for the job. These cost very little and maybe nothing at all if you ask around. Do any of your friends knit? They may have lots of spare needles and balls of yarn they can donate to get you going.

Otherwise, if none can be found for free, buy a pair of medium length knitting needles. Size 4mm is a good size to learn with.

You will also need some yarn. Find or buy some 'double knitting' yarn. This is a universal weight of yarn that is easy to knit with.

Side Note

To prove to yourself you're serious about your new hobby, choose a nice basket or simply use a plastic bag to keep your tools and knitting in.

Other useful tools:

- a tape measure (a metre length is sufficient)
- a small fairly sharp pair of scissors
- a darning needle

If you haven't got a tape measure, a ruler works well for measuring small pieces of work.

Basic Skills

Step One

So, armed with a ball of double knitting yarn, a pair of knitting needles (size 4mm) and a comfy chair, let's get going.

Make a slip knot approx. 30cm from the end of yarn and slip this on to one needle. This will be your first stitch.

Now with your right hand, push the other needle up through this slip knot and then hold both needles in your left hand.

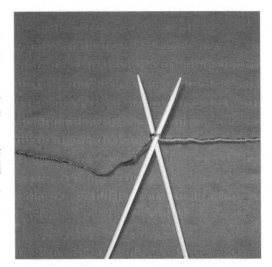

With your right hand, wind yarn from the main ball round the back of the right-hand needle and through the middle of the two needles towards you. (The yarn will be 'resting' on the front and back loop of the slip stitch.)

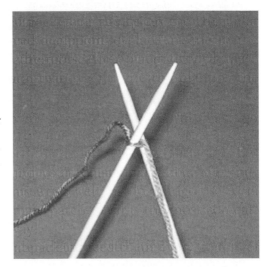

Hold this yarn gently with the left-hand needle in your left hand. With your right hand move the point of the right-hand needle down through the centre of the two needles and on the left side of the yarn you just placed.

Now pick up this yarn by keeping a circular clockwise movement of your right hand and letting go slightly of the yarn in your left hand.

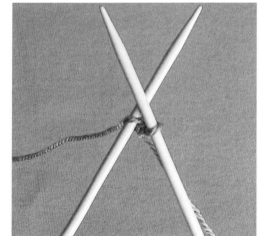

Now you should have a slip stitch on both needles. Slip the point of the left-hand needle under the stitch on the right-hand needle and pull it on to the left-hand needle.

Now you should have 2 stitches on the left-hand needle! Phew.

You now have two stitches!

*Pass the point of the right-hand needle between these stitches, under the left-hand needle.

Hold both needles with your left hand and wind yarn round the point of the right hand needle. Turn right-hand needle down to the left and pick up the stitch on to the right-hand needle. Then pass this stitch to the other needle.*

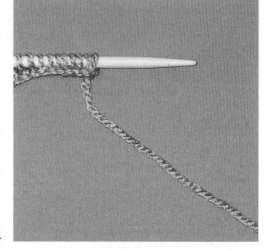

Now repeat this last stage from * to * until you have the required amount of stitches.

Rather than always pointing the needle upwards when you pass it through the stitches, try and point your needles towards each other at an angle. This will make your knitting easier to hold and you will have more control over the tension.

Now you can start knitting. You have just learned the most complicated affair of the whole process of knitting. Now you have this under your belt, the sky's the limit!

Knitting is really only a collection of slip knots slipped together in the right way. So let's knit your first few stitches.

Hold the needle with the stitches in your left hand.

Push the other needle up through the front loop of the first stitch, wind yarn round the back of the needle and through the centre as before, and pick up that stitch on to the right-hand needle.

Now, instead of putting it back on to the left-hand needle as you did when casting on, gently pull off the first stitch from the left-hand needle and let it drop. (This stitch is now hardly more than a loop of yarn wound round the needle, after you have made a stitch from it.) Don't panic! As long as you only let this first stitch drop, you're OK.

Side Note

If you mess up here, just start again. The more you practise, the better you'll get.

You are making slip knots along a row, and if you take the stitches off the needle, you should be able to unravel your knitting by simply pulling the yarn gently from the main ball. If you can do this easily you are getting it right. If the work knots or gets tangled before the last couple of stitches, you're going wrong somewhere.

Knit all the stitches in your row, then pass the needle with the stitches into your left hand and knit another row!

This stitch is known as 'garter' stitch. When you've mastered this basic stitch

you really are on the road to making your own clothes, toys and anything else that could possibly be knitted. Everything you learn from now on is just a variation on the basic stitch!

Take the stitches off your needle and pull gently on the yarn from the main ball while holding your work in your left hand. Does it unravel easily? Great!

If not, practise until it does!

Exercise

Don't wait to be an expert . . . start creating right now!

Most items of knitting require their cast-on edge be fairly firm – not tight and pulled together, just firm.

Here's how to create a firm edge.

Cast on some stitches, then on your first 'knit' row, knit every stitch into the back of the stitch, instead of the front.

When you look at the stitch on the needle, you see the front of the loop, where you have been pushing the other needle up through, and the back of the loop.

To create your firm edge, push the needle through the back loop instead of the front, over the top of the front of the stitch, wind yarn round as before, make the new stitch on your other needle and let the front of the stitch drop as before.

This little trick will give you a firmer edge every time!

Now back to the exercise: a knitted square!

You will need one pair of size 4mm knitting needles and approximately 20 metres of double knitting yarn.

Cast on 20 stitches and knit 36 rows.

If you get to four or five rows, and it doesn't look even, start again. The more you practise this bit, the quicker you will find the tension that's agreeable to you. Some people knit quite tightly, others loosely. The best way is the middle way! But overall consistency is the key. Keep practising to get your tension right.

When you need to stop, put your work down at the end of a row. If you leave it in the middle of a row it's very easy to lose stitches, and you could also get an uneven result.

To keep track of your rows, you can mark them down on a scrap of paper. If all the pens

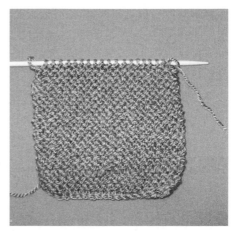

A 4-inch knitted square

regularly go walkabout in your house – as they do in mine – learn to count the rows!

Count each curly line as one row, ignoring the cast on edge. Remember to count both sides. After 36 rows, you will have 18 curly lines on each side!

With double knitting wool and 4mm needles, a square knitted with 20 stitches and 36 rows should come out at 4in (10cm) square.

Step Two

As with all things, the beginning sometimes seems slow, but don't give up now. You've done the hardest part.

In step two we are going to tackle how to cast off your stitches, and how to increase and decrease so that you can shape your work.

Complete the exercise in Step One and now work the cast-off row.

Knit the first two stitches in your row.

Using the point of the left-hand needle, lift the first stitch you knitted over the top of the second one and take it off the needle. You should have one stitch on the right-hand needle.

Knit the next stitch in the row, and again with the point of the left-hand needle, lift the second stitch over the third and take the second stitch right off the needle.

Always take the bottom stitch over the top of the stitch you have just knitted.

Carry on in this way until you have only one stitch left. Cut the yarn, leaving about 30cm, and thread through the last stitch. Pull gently but firmly to form the final knot.

When you've knitted two stitches, pick up the first stitch with the left-hand needle and lift it over the other stitch and off the needle.

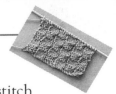

Gently pull stitch and yarn until firm on the needle. Then knit another stitch and repeat the process.

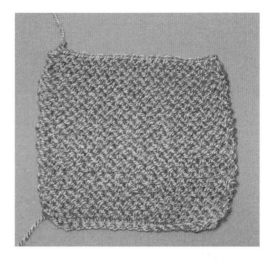

This is how the piece looks when four stitches have been cast off.

And this is the 4-inch square finished.

Side Note

You now have a small knitted square. Make lots in different colours and sew them together to produce blankets, cot covers, patchwork style bags and scarves, even cushion covers!

The next step is learning how to decrease stitches.

If a pattern requires more than one stitch to be removed in one row, you will normally be instructed to cast off a number of stitches. You do this as in normal casting off. (Details above.)

Often a pattern will tell you to knit two stitches together or K2tog.

This is straightforward but, as usual, requires a little practice.

Instead of pushing your needle up through the front of the first stitch to knit it, push it up through the second *and* first stitch on the needle.

Knit these two stitches as if they were one, therefore you will only transfer one stitch but will let the first two loops drop from the left-hand needle when you have made the new stitch on the right hand-needle.

Try this exercise (allow approx. 10 metres of yarn):

Cast on 20 stitches.

Knit your rows as usual, but knit two stitches together at the beginning of every row.

When you have only two stitches left, knit these two stitches together then cut the yarn, leaving about 20–30cm and thread it through the last stitch. Pull up gently but firmly.

Push the right-hand needle up through two stitches at once and knit as if one stitch.

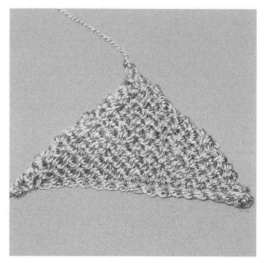

Voila! A triangle.

Side Note

You could be making patchwork blankets from triangles as well as squares, or a mixture of both. Start now. It's great fun!

Blanket stitch or oversew the pieces together using a darning needle and matching yarn, or use a contrasting colour.

Now we can get to grips with increasing stitches.

Of course to increase the number of stitches in a row, you can simply cast on a few, and sometimes a pattern will require you to do this.

Be careful to knit the new stitches through the back loops, though, or you may get a floppy edge or, even worse, a hole.

Practise this method by knitting a few rows – then before you knit the next row, cast on an extra six or eight stitches. Knit these stitches first – always into the back of each stitch, and also knit the first stitch of the existing stitches through the back of the loop. Check it out – practise!

To increase one stitch in the usual sense, do the following (NB: in a knitting pattern this will often be written as 'Inc.1' or 'Inc. 1st:'

Knit the first stitch as normal *but* before you let the loop drop off the needle,

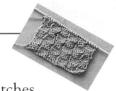

knit into it again through the back of the loop, so then you have two stitches for the price of one.

You knit into the front of the stitch, then into the back of the stitch before you let the loop escape the needle.

Knit into the front of the stitch.

Then into the back.

Now that you have two stitches on the right-hand needle, let the first loop on the left-hand needle drop. Gently pull to shape.

Practise increasing stitches with this exercise (allow approx. 10 metres of yarn). Cast on two stitches.

Increase in the first stitch and knit the other one.

Now you have three stitches.

On the next row, increase in the first stitch and knit the other two.

Carry on like this until you have 30 stitches.

Now you have an identical triangle to the one you made in the 'decreasing' exercise.

Side Note

Keep practising. Design a patchwork blanket – make it fairly small to start with! – and place triangles in the middle and squares around the edge. Choose blending colours or go for a totally random effect. Be on the lookout for balls of wool, or even hand-knitted jumpers you can un-pick.

Step Three

Step Three deals with the 'purl' stitch.

The purl stitch is important to learn so as to get that smooth knitted look most of us are used to – stocking stitch.

The term stocking stitch or stockinette stitch, as it's known in the US, refers to one knit row and one purl row repeated throughout the work.

The purl stitch also enables us to knit ribbed cuffs and textured patterns.

Are you sitting comfortably . . .? Let's go!

How to Purl

Cast on 20 stitches and knit one row. You don't need to knit this first row into the back of the stitches, but you can do – it's all good practice.

Now, with the needle with the stitches in your left hand, push the right hand needle down and to the left through the first stitch.

Wind the yarn round the tip of the right-hand needle, bring the needle back out of the stitch, and keeping a circular anti-clockwise movement, pick up the yarn you have wound round as you go.

Once you have the first stitch on the right-hand needle, let the first loop on the left-hand needle drop.

Carry on in this way until you have purled all the stitches in the row.

This may seem slightly impossible at first – but keep trying. Angle your needles, get comfortable holding the work, relax and try again.

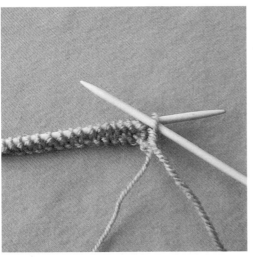

Push the right-hand needle down and to the left through the first stitch on the left-hand needle.

Wind yarn round tip of needle.

Keeping an anti-clockwise movement, pick up stitch on to right-hand needle and let the loop on the left-hand needle drop.

When you have purled a row, knit the next row, then purl another row.

You will see you have the regular knitted cloth 'look' – zigzag lines on one side and close together curly lines on the reverse. Purling is, in fact, just knitting backwards – well, almost.

NB: when you count your rows, you will only count the curly lines on the reverse side of the work. These represent every row you've knitted or purled.

Side Note

The 'zigzag line' side is the right side of your work (the side you see) and the 'curly' lines are the wrong side (or inside of your work).

When you knit a row, the right side of your work will be facing you, and when you purl a row, the 'wrong' side of your work will be facing you.

Try these Exercises

Make another 4-inch knitted square:

- cast on 24 stitches
- knit one row, purl one row until you have worked 28 rows
- then cast off

Try the triangle shape as well. Start with 24 stitches. Knit one row, purl one row, and decrease one stitch at the beginning of every row.

To decrease stitches when you are purling a row, simply pick up the first two stitches and purl them together.

To increase a stitch purlwise, purl into the front of the stitch and before you let the stitch drop, purl into the back of the same stitch.

A stocking-stitch square.

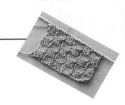

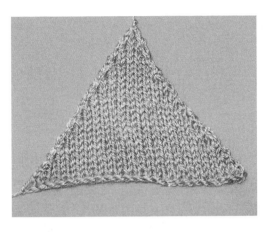

And a triangle!

Practise, practise, practise!

Side Note

You should be developing a feel for the tools you're working with now. Make it easy on yourself and find the method that suits you best.

Everyone has their own way of doing things and how you hold your needles and yarn will depend on many things, including the dexterity of your fingers.

Some knitters wind yarn round their needles using the third and fourth fingers of their right hand. Personally I've never mastered this method – although I believe it probably makes for faster knitting.

Use the method that suits you best.

By the time you've made a square using stocking stitch, i.e. knit one row, purl one row, you will have all the information you need to create any number of fancy stitches.

All knitting revolves around these two stitches:

- Knit: the creation of slip knots from slip knots all the way through the row
- Purl: creation of slip knots from slip knots, through the back of the work, all the way through the row

These two stitches are the only ones you will ever need.

Fancy knitting (lacework, cable, bobble patterns etc.) is only a combination of these two stitches, with decreasing and increasing thrown in for variety or shaping!

127

Make a few squares and triangles to get the hang of purling and then try this exercise:

Cast on 16 stitches.

First row: knit into the back of the stitches all along the row.

*Next row: knit 4 stitches. Then bring the yarn forward from the back of your work to the front through the middle of the two needles.

Now purl 4 stitches. Then pass the yarn back through the middle of the needles to the back of your work and knit 4 more stitches, then bring it back to the front and purl the last 4 stitches.

Repeat the last row three more times.

Next row: purl 4 stitches, knit 4 stitches, purl 4 stitches, knit 4 stitches. Remember to pass the yarn to the back to knit stitches and to the front to purl stitches.

Repeat the last row three more times.*

Now work from * to * once more.

Cast off stitches.

This is called basket stitch, and you can vary the pattern very simply with a little maths!

Each pattern sequence in the above example is 8 stitches (knit 4 stitches, purl 4 stitches) and in a row of 16 stitches this sequence would be repeated twice.

If you have 64 stitches on your row, divide 8 into 64. If it works, the pattern will. 8 x 8 = 64. So you will repeat the pattern of 8 stitches 8 times through the row.

Basket stitch

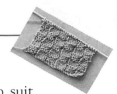

You can also change the number of stitches in each pattern sequence to suit yourself.

For example, with 16 stitches on the needles, you could knit two stitches, then purl two stitches for four rows then purl two stitches and knit two stitches for four rows.

This brings us nicely to 'ribbing'.

Often the bottom edge, neckband and cuffs of a jumper are knitted in rib to produce more elasticity in the garment.

To create normal, everyday rib stitch, you simply knit one stitch then purl one stitch along the row. Don't forget to bring your yarn forward to purl, and back to knit.

Don't swap round to produce basket stitch as above – just keep doing the same stitch for however many rows the pattern asks for.

To create double rib, knit two stitches, purl two stitches etc. and I guess triple rib must be knit three stitches, purl three stitches.

Single rib

Try this out!

Make some wrist and ankle warmers for someone you love! Whether they're at their computer, driving the kids to school or in the garden, these nifty little accessories will keep them cosy and warm on frosty winter mornings and can be knitted in no time.

Wrist and ankle warmers
NB: wrist and ankle warmers are made entirely in single rib, i.e. knit one stitch, purl one stitch in every row.
You will need:
1 pair of 6½mm needles
50 grams of 'chunky' yarn or use 2 strands together of double knitting yarn

To Make Wrist Warmers

Cast on 18 stitches (fairly loosely).
Work 18 rows of knit one, purl one, rib.
Cast off.
To make up: sew row ends together.

To Make Ankle Warmers

Cast on 24 stitches (fairly loosely).
Work 24 rows of knit one, purl one, rib.
Cast off.
To make up: sew row ends together.

Side Note

Experiment. Instead of using chunky yarn, try knitting with three or four strands of lighter yarn together. Use blending colours, or whatever you have available!

If your wrist or ankle warmers come up the wrong size, you will need to undo and start again . . . don't worry – these are quick to make and good to practise on!

If the end result is too small, add another strand or two.

If the end result is too large, take out a strand or two.

Keep ribbing firm but not tight.

Step Four

Before we get on to Step Four, I have to emphasise the need to practise. As with any new undertaking, knitting can seem difficult at first. If you keep practising, you will find the best way for you, and eliminate all those 'that's impossible' and 'I can't get my fingers to do that!' thoughts. Practise but don't overdo your sessions.

Knitting is a great hobby to fill in five or ten minutes here and there.

Side Note

I have been known to keep my knitting in a voluminous pocket and knit a couple of rows while I'm standing in the kitchen watching the dinner but that's just obsessive!

However, it does stop me from trying out the food too often, and I can definitely lose weight more easily if I keep something bubbling on my knitting needles!

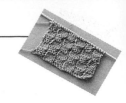

On to Step Four . . . Colour!

You will need at least two different-coloured yarns – both double knitting weight – and we will use the knitted square pattern to practise with.

Horizontal Stripes

Using one colour, we will call this your main colour (M), cast on 20 stitches.

Knit six rows as you did in the knitted square.

Now, to start a stripe with your contrast colour (C), make a loop about 20–30cm from the end of the yarn around the main colour and push it up to the last stitch you knitted.

Ignore your main colour, which should be sitting in the middle of your contrast colour loop.

Take the double thickness of contrast yarn and knit the first three stitches with the two strands.

Let the short end drop and knit the rest of the row with one strand of yarn.

Knit another row with the contrast yarn. Now before you knit the next row, wind the contrast yarn around the main colour yarn, then knit the row as normal. This will keep the main colour running up the side of your work and available for when you need it.

Knit another four rows, remembering to loop the colours after the second of these four rows.

Now after six rows of contrast, you can use the main colour again. Loop the colours again and carry on knitting with the main colour and let the contrast colour rest at the side of your work.

Knit six rows with the main colour, remembering to loop the colours together on every alternate row.

Carry on in this way until you have six stripes. Then cast off using whichever colour you prefer.

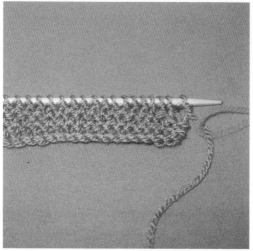

Wrap new colour around the main colour.

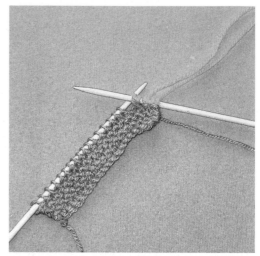

Knit the first three stitches with two strands of yarn.

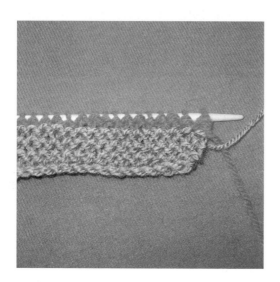

Twist colours at row end – don't pull tight.

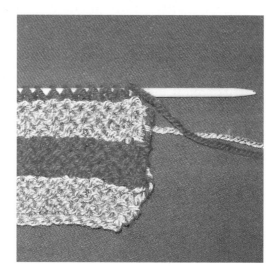

A stripy knitted square in progress.

Work a stocking-stitch square (knit one row, purl one row) in the same way.

Side Note

Practise making different squares with different combinations of colours or row numbers.

For example, you could knit six rows black and two rows white or four rows green and six rows red.

Keep your numbers even – i.e. two, four, six, eight, ten.

You will see that on the 'wrong' side of your work, there will be rows of two colours together. If you change your stripes to multiples of 'odd' numbers you will see these rows on both sides of your work.

Intarsia or Picture Knitting

This is more complicated but easy when you get the hang of it. Take this slowly and methodically and you will be delighted with your results!

Before you start, practise making some stripy squares using stocking stitch (one row knit, one row purl).

Intarsia knitting will invariably use stocking stitch.

The easiest way to get the feel of intarsia is with vertical stripes.

As before, you will need a main colour (M) and a contrast colour (C), both in double knitting weight yarn.

Using M cast on 25 stitches and purl the first row.

For the next row, knit five stitches. Then join on C by looping round the M as before in horizontal stripes. Knit three stitches with two strands of yarn, then let the short end drop. Knit two more stitches with C.

Leaving a couple of metres of the main colour, cut and join to C as before. Then repeat, knitting three stitches with two strands and two stitches with a single strand. Rejoin from the main ball to C and repeat as before. Knit three stitches with two strands, knit two more stitches.

Finally, cut C, leaving a couple of metres, and rejoin to M. Knit the first three stitches with two strands, let the short end drop and knit the last two stitches. The point of knitting the first three stitches, after changing colour, with two strands of yarn is to make a secure casting on.

Now you will have four long ends of yarn, which will probably get slightly tangled, but keep an eye on them! You can help keep your work neat by untangling the yarn after every row.

Now purl a row. Purl the first five stitches in M, then twist C round M, and purl five stitches in C. Then twist M round C and purl five stitches in M. Continue to the end of the row.

Keep practising this until you can change colours without creating holes in your work.

Your next row will be a knit row, then a purl row, and so on until you have got the hang of it.

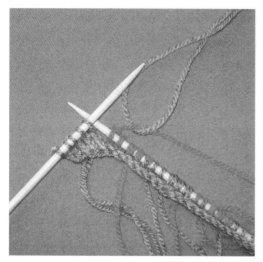
Join new colour along the row.

Twist colours together.

Vertical stripes!

To create pictures in your cloth, called intarsia, it is often easiest to work from a graph.

Try a simple heart shape.

NB: NR stands for Next Row, M stands for Main colour and C stands for Contrast colour.

With M, cast on 24 stitches.

Knit 5 rows.

Purl one row.

NR: Knit 11 stitches, leaving a few metres cut yarn. Join on C and knit two stitches, leave a few metres and cut the yarn. Rejoin M and knit 11 stitches.

NR: Purl 10 stitches, twist C round M and purl the next 4 stitches with C, twist second length of M round C and purl 10 stitches with M.

Remember to twist yarns when changing colour. Refer to the intarsia pictures.

NR: Knit 9M, knit 6C, knit 9M

NR: Purl 8M, purl 8C, purl 8M

NR: Knit 7M, knit 10C, knit 7M

NR: Purl 6M, purl 12C, purl 6M

NR: Knit 5M, knit 14C, knit 5M

NR: Purl 4M, purl 16C, purl 4M

NR: Knit 3M, knit 18C, knit 3M

NR: Purl 2M, purl 20C, purl 2M

NR: Knit 2M, knit 20C, knit 2M

NR: Purl 2M, purl 20C, purl 2M

NR: Knit 2M, knit 20C, knit 2M

NR: Purl 2M, purl 9C, leave a length of yarn, and cut. Join on a new length of M. Purl 2M. Cut yarn, leaving a length. Join C. Purl 9C. Cut yarn, join on M and purl last 2 stitches with M

NR: Knit 3M, knit 7C, knit 4M, knit 7C, knit 3M

NR: Purl 4M, purl 5C, purl 6M, purl 5C, purl 4M

Then continue with M.

Knit 1 row.

Purl 1 row.

Knit 4 rows and cast off.

If you prefer to work directly from a graph, here it is!

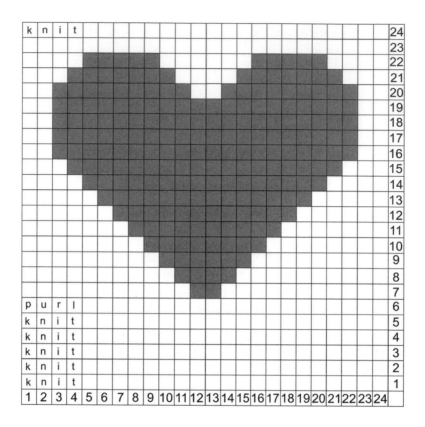

When working from a graph, all knit rows should be followed from right to left and purl rows from left to right.

Side Note

In Fair Isle designs, patterns of colours are repeated across the rows and colours are normally carried behind your work, rather than using lots of small balls or lengths of yarn.

This works well if you are colour changing every two or three stitches. With more than three stitches in one colour block, you will need to use separate balls or lengths of yarn to avoid pulling at the back of your work.

In cases such as black and white colour changes, you will certainly need to use separate lengths, otherwise when the black yarn is pulled across the back of a white block of stitching, it will show through.

Although lots of short lengths can be a nuisance, there are special spools you can buy to wind your yarn round. Take it slowly. Picture knitting is *not* as fast as regular knitting. Take your time after every row to untangle yarn and look at what you've done.

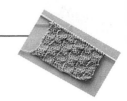

You can use your heart square in a patchwork blanket or cushion cover.

Design a few stripy squares and colourful hearts. Keep a patchwork blanket as an ongoing project. When you have a little yarn left over from another project, or you acquire a bag full of assorted balls, use them to add to the blanket. Experiment with textures as well as colours.

Well, that's just about all you need to begin with.

Try making things straight away. Don't worry if they're not perfect. You can always unpick and start again another day!

To stop you straying from your knitting path, here's a list of hints and tips and common abbreviations used.

Hints and Tips

Knit your first row into the back of each stitch for a firmer edge.

Keep stitches mobile on the needles. If they are too tight to move, you're either knitting too tightly or you have the yarn weight and needle size at the wrong ratio. Practise until your hands find a comfortable rhythm.

Sit in a comfortable chair with your back supported and stop for a break when your neck aches!

Experiment with shaping
Increase and decrease stitches at random. Jot down what you've done and then, if you like the effect, you'll be able to repeat it!

Make something useful or practical
Try the wrist and ankle warmers in Step Three.

Collect old hand-knitted garments and unpick them for the yarn
And of course collect all the ends you can. Check out charity shops for oddment bags, build a relationship with your local yarn supplier and try to get end of lines with a discount.

Forget the idea that knitting is a needlecraft
Treat it as a regular craft. You really can knit with broomsticks and fishing rope, or chopsticks and silk, although you don't *have* to . . .

When you attempt your first garment, choose an easy pattern
Read it through before you start and make sure you understand every word.

Try different joining methods
Blanket-stitch your small squares together or try crocheting them together – crocheting is much, much faster when you get the hang of it.

Try out different yarns and needle sizes to compare resulting textures
There are some stunning yarns available these days.

And here's a list of commonly used abbreviations:

K	Knit
P	Purl
st(s)	stitch(es)
K2tog	Knit two stitches together or purl two stitches together
P2tog	Purl two stitches together or purl two stitches together
NR	Next row
st.st	stocking stitch
inc	increase
dec	decrease

Knitting Patterns

Try out your knitting skills with a few simple patterns before attempting anything too difficult.

The Ekokids

The rag dolls in the following pages are made with very simple stitches and are easy to follow with step-by-step instructions. The Ekokids are teenage dolls without plastic accessories and you don't need a battery charger or a computer to play with them! Children, young and old, will adore them.

Make dolls from one basic pattern and choose the personality you want. Add your own unique design, by changing colours or stripes. Clothes can be mixed and matched and are removable.

Basic Doll Pattern

Head

(made in one piece)

> To make:
> cast on 8sts and purl one row
> st.st 6 rows, increasing 1st at each end of all 3 knit rows (14sts)
> st.st 8 rows
> st.st 4 rows, decreasing 1st at each end of both knit rows (10sts)
> st.st 4 rows, increasing 1st at each end of both knit rows (14sts)
> st.st 8 rows
> st.st 6 rows, decreasing 1st at each end of all 3 knit rows (8sts)
> cast off, leaving a 40cm length of yarn
>
> To make up:
> Fold in half with wrong sides together
> Oversew round edge leaving neck edge open
> Turn inside out so purl side is on the outside

Features

Using a darning needle, make small backstitches for eyes, nose and mouth. Fasten off yarn inside head.

> Tip: Mark the position of features with pins before sewing.
> Stuff head gently but firmly, leaving neck edge open.

Hair

Leaving long loops between stitches, backstitch hair in place. Start from the top and work 3 or 4 (or more) lines of hair across the back of the head. Cut all loops and trim hair.

Body and Arms
(made in one piece)
>To make:
>
>cast on 14sts and st.st 20 rows.
>
>NR: cast on 26sts then knit these 26sts, knit next stitch through back of stitch, knit 13sts
>
>NR: cast on 26sts, then purl these 26sts, purl next stitch through back of stitch, purl 39sts (66sts)
>
>St.st 4 rows
>
>NR: K29sts, cast off 8sts, knit to end
>
>NR: P29sts, turn work, cast on 8sts, turn work again and purl to end
>
>NR: K29sts, knit next stitch through back of stitch, K7sts, knit next stitch through back of stitch, knit to end
>
>St.st 3 rows, starting with a purl row
>
>NR: cast off 26sts, knit to end
>
>NR: cast off 26sts, purl to end (14sts)
>
>St.st 20 rows and cast off, leaving a length of yarn for sewing up.
>
>To make up:
>
>Fold in half with purl side outside. Oversew round arms and body, leaving neck edge and bottom edge open.
>
>Stuff gently but firmly.
>
>Tip: stuff the arms a little at a time as you sew, or use the blunt end of a pencil to push filling through length of arms after sewing.
>
>Pin the neck edge of the head into the neck opening of the body and back-stitch in place, pushing in more filling as needed.

Legs

(make two pieces)

Tip: when casting on or off, or knitting with more than one colour in a row, cross over different colours at the back of your work to avoid holes appearing. Keep it neat as this will be on the outside eventually.

>To make:
>
>Cast on 28sts with main body colour and 6 sts in shoe colour
>
>To make legs with high boots, cast on 20sts in body colour and 14sts in boot colour
>
>St.st 14 rows and cast off.
>
>To make up:
>
>Fold each leg in half with the purl side outside

Oversew, leaving the top edge open
Stuff gently but firmly.

Tip: Stuff the legs as you sew, a little at a time, or use the blunt end of a pencil to push stuffing through length of legs after sewing.

Pin both legs in place, just inside the bottom edge of body piece
    Oversew, or backstitch round each one, attaching firmly to the body, pushing in more filling as needed. Close the gap between the legs with a couple of stitches.
    So there you have it – your basic Ekokid!

The following instructions are for 'Baby' Ekokid. Read through the pattern before you start so you know what colours and other variations you need. Get adventurous and design your own characters. You could knit the basic doll in luminous green for a monster doll for instance!

Baby

Baby Ekokid was made with pink yarn for the basic doll and used 16 metres of yellow yarn for the hair.

Tip: use 4mm needles for all clothes and accessories.

Dress

    (made in two pieces using approx. 26metres of blue and 10metres of mauve yarn)
        To make:
        With mauve yarn, cast on 16sts and
            knit two rows
        Break mauve, join on blue and st.st
            22 rows
        NR: cast on 16sts, knit these 16sts,
            knit next stitch through back of
            stitch and knit to end
        NR: cast on 16sts, purl these 16sts,
            purl next stitch through back of
            stitch and purl to end (48sts)
        St.st 6 rows
        Break off blue, join mauve and knit 2
            rows. Cast off.

141

To make up:
Oversew side and sleeve seams.

Hat
(made in two pieces using approx. 12metres of mauve and 1metre of red yarn)
To make:
Cast on 28sts and knit 16 rows
NR: K1st, (K2sts together, K1st) to end
NR: Purl
Repeat last 2 rows two more times
Thread yarn through remaining 9sts, and fasten off.
To make up:
Oversew row ends together.

Flower
With red yarn, cast on 5sts, knit 1 row and cast off.
Join row ends and attach to hat.

Waistcoat
(made in one piece using approx. 15metres of blue/grey yarn)
To make:
Cast on 32sts and st.st 10 rows
NR: K6sts, K2sts together, turn and work on these 7sts
Starting with a purl row, st.st 5 rows
NR: K2sts together, knit to end
Purl to last 2sts, P2sts together
Repeat these last 2 rows once more. Cast off last 3sts
Rejoin yarn. K2sts together, K12sts, K2sts together. Turn and work on these
    14sts
Starting with a purl row, st.st 9 rows. Cast off
Rejoin yarn. K2sts together, K6sts
Starting with a purl row, st.st 5 rows
NR: Knit to last 2sts, K2 together
NR: P2sts together, purl to end
Repeat last 2 rows once more. Cast off last 3sts.
To make up:
Oversew shoulder and side seams.

Backpack
(made in two pieces using approx. 15 metres of pink yarn)

To make main piece:
Cast on 10sts, knit 40 rows and cast off.

Strap

Cast on 70sts and cast off.

To make up:

Fold bag in three lengthwise and oversew side seams, leaving flap at top.

Pin centre of strap to centre bottom of bag.

Oversew strap to bag along bottom edge and up both sides. Then backstitch ends of strap to each bottom corner of bag, to form shoulder straps.

Dress your doll and create a change of clothes and matching accessories for her next night out!

A Fluffy Scarf and a French Beret

The following two items are made using spider stitch. Spider stitch is easy to do.

How to Spider Stitch

Push the needle up through the first stitch. Wind yarn round *both* needles.

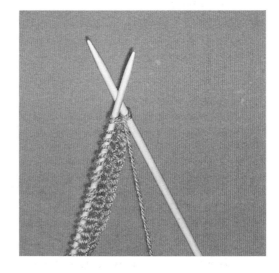

Then wind yarn round the right-hand needle and knit the stitch.

Allow the loop to fall and make your next stitch.

The stitches will be very loose on your right-hand needle so watch they don't fall off the end.

Pull the work gently into shape every few stitches.

Practise a little to get the feel of the knitting then try these two easy items.

A Fluffy Scarf

You need a pair of size 4mm needles and about 75–100grams of funky knit yarn. Funky yarns are fun to knit with once you get the hang of them. Choose a soft and stringy type for your scarf.

    To make:

    Cast on 30 stitches and knit one row. Work in spider stitch until the scarf
        is the length you require. Knit one row then cast off.

You can work the scarf in double spider stitch, which is simply winding the yarn around the needle twice instead of once before knitting the stitch. The scarf will grow faster but the 'holes' will be larger.

A French Beret

This resembles a typical crochet French beret but it's knitted!

Materials

   1 pair of 10mm needles
   50grams of chunky yarn

   To make:

   Using one strand of yarn throughout, cast on 50sts and knit 2 rows. Work the following 2 pattern rows 4 times:

   Pattern row 1: double spider stitch

   Pattern row 2: knit

   NR: (double spider stitch 3sts, double spider stitch 2sts together) 10 times (40sts)

   NR: (Knit 2sts, knit 2sts together) 10 times (30sts)

   NR: (double spider stitch 1st, double spider stitch 2 sts together) 10 times (20sts)

   NR: (knit 2sts together) 10 times (10sts)

   Break yarn and thread through the remaining stitches. Pull up tight and fasten off securely. Sew the side seam. If required, a narrow piece of elastic can be threaded through the base of the hat, so it stays on the head without the use of hair clips or hatpins.

Part Four

In the Nursery

Pencil and Paper Games

Before the days of computer games and PlayStations, children were obliged to make their own entertainment. Most of us, who can remember back that far, spent our childhood years playing outside even if it was raining! Sometimes. Then, if we were so inclined and lucky enough to have them, we may have enjoyed a jigsaw puzzle or a board game. But there were moments when a pencil and a piece of paper were the only equipment needed to amuse us all.

These games still entertain today – albeit often in the form of a computer game!

Battleships

The pencil and paper version of battleships has been a family favourite since before the First World War! There are lots of variations, and the game can be adapted to suit the age of the child and level of difficulty required.

To play the traditional game of battleships you will need:

- 2 players
- 2 fairly large sheets of paper – A4 size is fine or use graph paper if available
- a pencil or pen for each player

Draw two grids on each sheet of paper ten squares by ten squares. Number the squares from 1–10 along the top of each grid and label the rows as letters A–J along one side from top to bottom.

On one grid, the player marks his or her own ships, and records which ones the opponent has hit. And on the other, each player records in which squares he or she has chosen to make an attack on his opponent.

Before the game starts, the players mark down where their ships are situated – this must be kept secret from the other player.

Ships must be marked in a continuous line either vertically or horizontally on the grid. The initial of each ship is placed within the squares.

Create on your grid:

1 aircraft carrier (A) – using 5 squares
1 battleship (B) – using 4 squares
1 cruiser (C) – using 3 squares
1 destroyer (D) – 3 squares
1 submarine (S) – 2 squares

Write this list down on a postcard or another sheet of paper and keep in view of both players or make a note of it on each sheet of playing paper.

Now both players should have a sheet of paper with two 10x10 grids and all their secret ships marked down on one of them.

This is an example of how your grid should look before starting to play. The other grid will be empty.

	1	2	3	4	5	6	7	8	9	10
A										
B	C				D	D	D			S
C	C									S
D	C									
E										
F									B	
G		A	A	A	A	A			B	
H									B	
I									B	
J										

Player One starts and chooses at random any square he wants to try and 'hit' one of his opponent's ships. He may call out G7. If Player Two has a ship covering that space she must say HIT. If she hasn't, it's a MISS. On his empty grid, Player One marks off what the result was. A miss can be marked as an M or an X and a hit marked as either an H or a tick ✓. Player Two then takes her turn and chooses a square to try and hit one of her opponent's ships. If Player Two hits a ship, she marks it on her opponent's grid so he knows which square has been hit because, when the whole ship has been sunk, a player has to declare which ship it was and that it has been sunk. A player, for example, might say, 'Hit and sunk my aircraft carrier!' Whoever sinks all the opponent's ships first is the winner.

Variations
The grids can be larger and more ships entered.

When a player makes a hit, the owner of the ship can say which ship it is and then the opponent knows how many squares he is looking for.

Remember, the squares must be in a line horizontally or vertically, and must not overlap.

More than one square can be called at a time. You may wish to hit three squares in each turn. As long as each player has an equal number of choices, five or six can be chosen at once.

Consequences

This is another pencil and paper game that can be adapted according to the ages of the players. An adult version can be played after the kids have gone to bed!

Each player will need a piece of paper and a pen or pencil. Cut A4 sheets of paper in half lengthwise and give one piece to each player. Any number of players can play at once. The more the merrier.

The Picture Version

Each player draws a picture of a head and neck at the top of his paper. He must keep the drawing secret. Make the neck slightly longer and then fold over the paper twice to hide the drawing but leave small marks where the neck finishes. The papers are then passed to the next player in the circle or on your left. Then each player draws a body on the new piece of paper but must *not* look at the head that has been drawn by the previous player.

Again, the paper should be folded twice and a little mark put where the lower part of the body ends for the next player to join on to. The papers are then passed on again and each player draws two legs, folding and leaving marks as before. Finally all players draw the feet. Then all players fold over their papers, pass them to the next player, and everyone opens their drawings to find the strangest muddled up monsters, animals or people you have ever seen!

The Written Version

The same principle applies – after each turn the paper must be folded and passed on. The first thing to write is a name – a male name perhaps. Fold and pass on. The next thing on the list is another name but before that you must write 'met'.

Next write: 'he said to her' – and then write anything he could have said to her. Fold and pass on.

Next write: 'she said to him' – write what she may have said.

Next write: 'then he' – write what he may have done.

Next write: 'then she' – write what she may have done.

Then write: 'and the consequence of this story is . . .' and finish off the story – for example 'they both climbed a tree.'

Fold and pass on, then everyone opens the papers and reads them out loud.

If adults are playing, rules apply according to the mood of the moment!

Tip: use paper clips to hold folds in place, before passing the piece of paper to the next player.

Boxes

Boxes can be played on a chalkboard, a piece of paper, or even outside on the patio on a fine day. Draw lines of dots and take turns in joining just two of the dots together. How many lines of dots you draw is up to you and how much space you have. When someone completes a box – puts the fourth line in place – they put their initial in the box and have another turn.

Players can only join two adjacent dots on each turn, unless they complete a box.

When all the dots have been joined and all the boxes are complete, count up the initials. The one with the most boxes is the winner.

Play a giant version of this on a patio or any smooth outside surface using chalk. Use a broom to sweep away the lines when the game is over.

Boy's Name, Girl's Name . . .

This is a fun game but educational too. Age groups don't matter as long as the players are able to read and write to a reasonable standard.

Each player has a sheet of paper and a pencil or pen. Copy the following table on to each sheet of paper.

Letter	A		B		C		D	
Boy's name								
Girl's name								
Fruit								
Vegetable								
Colour								
Country								
Animal								
Flower								
	Total		Total		Total		Total	

The letters of the alphabet can be any letters chosen by the players. They don't have to be in alphabetical order.

Each player fills in, under the 'Letter' column, a boy's name beginning with the letter specified and so on. For example, a player may fill in the following list for the letter A:

andrew

alison

apricot

asparagus

amber

australia

antelope

aster

When all players have finished one column, everyone calls out their answers. A player who has an answer that no other player has receives two points and puts a two in the small column next to the answer he has given. If more than one player has the same answer, all those players receive one point. If no answer could be found, the player gets no score for that category. Add the column of numbers to find the winner.

Variations

Other subjects can be used instead of or as well as the above list. Choose the ones you all like to play with.

tree or shrub

herb or flower

town or country

animal or bird

or even:

film stars

singers

games

TV programmes

The choice is yours!

Fun Family Games

To make a change from pencil and paper games, these indoor games are fun for the family and children's parties and they can also be played outside on a dry day. Very little equipment is needed, if any. All that is needed are willing players who are prepared to have a bit of fun!

Chinese Whispers

No equipment needed.

Why this is called 'Chinese' whispers, I have no idea. I suppose those of us who played in the West many years ago considered Chinese to be a language that made no sense to us at all. This game can end up making no sense at all!

Position as many players as possible in a circle or comfortably around a playing area. They should all be sitting. One person is chosen to be the first player and has to think of a sentence. It can be anything at all – for example, 'The cat slept under the table.' The more words there are, the better, but it must be one sentence only. The player then whispers this sentence to the next player. He or she must only say it once and no one else must hear. The second player then whispers what he or she thought they heard to the next player in the circle.

If any player at any time doesn't catch all of the sentence, they must whisper to the next player, what they *thought* they heard. The sentence must never be repeated twice to one player. When all players have heard the whisper, the last person before the one who started the whisper says out loud what he believed he heard from the player before.

Then the person who started it must state what the original sentence was. The more players, the more variations you get, and the starting phrase can be very different from the ending one!

This can be played outside and players don't have to sit in a circle. As long as every gets a turn in the right order, players can be scattered all over the house and garden!

Hide the Thimble

You will need:

a small object to hide

Hide the thimble has been played for generations, and although many households do not even possess a thimble, the game can be still be enjoyed today. Choose a small object and show it to all the players. Then the players must go into another room and not peep until the object has been hidden by an adult or a chosen player.

The players must come back in and search for the object but must replace everything they move exactly as it was before they moved it. A few clues can be given. Players can ask the person who hid the object whether they are 'hot', 'cold' or 'warm'.

'Hot' is very close to the hidden object, 'warm' is fairly close and 'cold' is far away. Once a player has had a 'hot' answer, all players will be rushing to the point and searching there.

The person who finds the 'thimble' is the winner and can be the one who hides it the next time, or the one who wins a prize if the game is played as a party game.

This game is also played by many families at Easter time. Hunt the Easter egg has long been a favourite on Easter Sunday morning with the children. Hide lots of small eggs all over the house and garden, then let the children loose – but try and get them to eat breakfast first!

A–Z

You will need:

counters or small pieces of paper

This is another fun game to play with adults and children who are able to read or at least know the first letter of a word. All players sit in a circle and a subject is chosen, such as 'animals'. One player starts and has to name an animal beginning with the letter A. The next player has to name an animal with the letter B, and so on. If a player cannot think of an animal with that letter, he gets a point – or a token from the middle of the circle (these can be counters, or simply circles or squares of paper). Then the next player has to try and think of an animal with the letter not yet found. If all the players cannot think of one, then the letter is skipped and play continues with the next letter in the alphabet.

After each round – from A–Z – points are added up and the player with the fewest points is the winner. Each time a round is played, the next player in the circle should start. This game can be played with as few as two players but more is always merrier!

Storytelling

No equipment needed.

This is a good game to fire the imagination. Any number of players can play although it's more fun with more than two players. One person starts telling a story of his or her choice. The player should say a few sentences and stop, leaving an open-ended line, such as 'she said' or 'and they went to'. The next player continues the story, changing the plot and bringing in new characters if he or she wants to.

The game can go on all night or until the possibilities have been exhausted or players are bored! Start a new story at any time. Keeping the story flowing but bringing in all sorts of twists and turns will make the game more fun. Different age groups can play, but older players should be careful not to make it too complicated for the younger ones.

Rainy-Day Crafts

Spend some quality time with the kids and get down to some sticking and painting! These ideas will keep young and old busy for hours – and not a plug or a battery in sight.

Mosaics

You can decorate exercise books, cards or just make stand-alone pictures with mosaic craft. Collect lots of coloured paper. This can be from packaging or magazines, as long as it is more or less the same weight (although you could use different thicknesses of paper to produce different textures). But to begin making mosaics, keep it fairly simple and easy to handle.

Cut the coloured paper into small squares, up to 1cm by 1cm in size. Keep different colours together. A few matchboxes or other suitable containers can be used to keep the small pieces safe.

The materials you will need for mosaic craft are:
> coloured paper
> matchboxes or other containers
> scissors
> paper glue
> pencils and paper

Draw a picture on a piece of paper or cover of an exercise book and glue the small squares of coloured paper in place. Overlap slightly or push the pieces very close together so you don't get gaps. Use a different colour for each part of the picture and fill in as if you were painting by numbers. Or, if you prefer, make a random picture of colours with the squares of coloured paper.

When you get the hang of mosaic craft, try all sorts of decorating techniques:

- change the shape of your mosaic pieces
- decorate exercise books
- decorate display boxes and matchboxes – the containers used for the coloured squares can be covered in the corresponding colour
- use different thicknesses of paper
- add a sequin or two or a little glitter to bring a sparkle to your picture
- stick a cloth border around the edge to add texture to your pictures

Magazine Envelopes

Magazines with advertising pages covering a whole page make great envelopes! Tear or cut the whole page out of the magazine and fold into an envelope shape. Use glue or Sellotape to seal the edges. Cut a piece of white paper to stick to the front of the envelope to write the address on. These envelopes are fun and colourful and can bring a smile to a postie's face on a cold winter morning!

Papier Mâché

Papier mâché is a wonderful modelling medium and can be made simply at home with everyday ingredients. It is a bit messy so covered surfaces and aprons are advisable! Use a plastic tablecloth.

Make all sorts of elaborate models, masks, decorations, even bowls and plates. The main ingredient is paper so unless many coats of varnish have been applied to the finished model, meticulously covering every centimetre, the finished article won't be waterproof and should not be immersed in water.

You will need:
        newspapers
        adhesive
        a paintbrush
        emulsion paint to seal
        paints to finish

Also you will need:

an object for casting your creation, such as a dish or a balloon

Vaseline, cooking oil or washing-up liquid

The adhesive you use can be any good paper glue. Wallpaper paste is excellent because it usually has a fungicide which protects your finished model against damp and mould. It should be made up according to the packet. However, if you are making papier mâché with young children, wallpaper paste could get into their mouths and eyes, so a more child-friendly paste is better.

Make a flour and water glue by boiling water in a pan. Mix flour with a little cold water in a basin to form a paste and then add to the pan. Stir well and simmer gently for a few minutes. The more flour you use, the thicker the glue will be.

To start modelling you will need to protect your mould so that the item you are making can be taken off without breaking when finished. Smear Vaseline, cooking oil or washing-up liquid over the surface you will be covering. Clingfilm can be used or simple strips of wet paper, soaked in water – not glue. Balloons don't need anything applied to them. When the papier mâché has dried, the balloon can be burst and will come away easily.

When you have your mould ready, prepare the paper.

Tear the newspaper into strips about 1in (2.5cms) by 4in (10cms). The measurements don't have to be exact. Tear the lengths along the grain of the paper.

Paste the strips on both sides with the adhesive, and stick them to the prepared surface. Smooth down to press out any air bubbles. Lay on a few layers over the whole surface. Leave to dry. Add as many layers as you want to but do so a few at a time, or the finished item will take too long to dry right through and could start to go mouldy before it has dried.

If you want to add a decoration, or a handle, make the required shape out of card and stick it to the object with masking tape. Cover with layers of glued paper as before.

When the paper is totally dry, carefully remove the mould. Paint with two coats of emulsion paint to seal and then decorate with other colours as required.

Box-Land

Let your imagination run wild and climb into the world of cardboard boxes!

How many of us have experienced the delight in giving a small child a brand new toy, only to find he or she really does prefer the box it came in? Well, two can play at that game! Welcome to the world of cardboard box-land where anything may happen! Let your imagination run wild and spend some quality time with the little darlings as well.

Collect cardboard boxes; cereal packets, paper plates or anything cardboard will be useful.

Keep advertising brochures, old catalogues and magazines.

Look out for unusual textures or patterns in used wrapping paper and packaging.

Don't throw away small pieces of cloth or ribbon. They are great for trimmings, adding that finishing touch!

Tip: collect all this in the biggest of the boxes. It's surprising how much less your garbage will be at the end of the week!

Alongside all these recycled goodies you will need:

        pencils, markers, crayons etc.
        a decent pair of scissors
        glue and adhesive tape

Trains and Boats and Cars

Make whichever your child happens to be into at the moment! The one problem with this idea is that you really do need a strong back as you'll no doubt be expected to provide engine power when the vehicle is built.

Use a large box for the main body of the vehicle, making sure your child can sit in it comfortably. With child-safe paper fasteners, attach paper plates to resemble wheels and a steering wheel or cut circles from card and attach with a length of wool taken through the centre.

Make a windscreen from another box or piece of card by cutting a window in it and glueing it to the main body.

Add extra 'carriages' on a train by tying smaller boxes behind the main one. These carry the passengers (teddies or other favourite toys).

Draw symbols or pictures with a thick marker and, finally, colour or paint it.

Optional extra! An engine needs horse power and, as you'll be the horse, you'll need some reins. A fairly sturdy length of rope attached through the front of the vehicle should do it. Now pull your tiny one round in their train to their heart's delight!

Castles or Dream Homes

For the main body you will need a very large box or two placed together. Either works well as the 'castle' doesn't get pulled about, we hope.

Glue painted cereal packets turret-style around the box. If the box is fairly high (make sure your child can't fall by leaning on the side), cut out some windows. Add curtains by sticking a scrap of material on the inside.

'Wallpaper' the inside walls with pictures from old catalogues and magazines, and paint the outside.

A circle of blue cloth on the floor outside the castle or house serves well as a moat or pond. Cut out brightly coloured fish shapes and scatter them in the 'water'.

Theatres and Televisions

Cut or remove half of the base of a regular sized box. Turn the box on to one short side with the gap facing outwards. The gap created by the piece removed is where the stage will be set.

Decorate the theatre lavishly with shiny paper, ribbons and bows etc.

Hang a length of cloth over the back of the box (originally the open top) to hide the puppeteer.

Then hold your own puppet show! Cut celebrity pictures from magazines and stick them on to thin card. Attach a length of card or a smooth stick to manoeuvre them with. Make up a script and see who can say with it without laughing! See the puppets section on p. 163 for more ideas on making different types of puppets.

Un-armed Bandits!

Turn a medium-sized box on its longest edge and, on the inside of this edge, draw 'target' areas. These could simply be strips of different colours with numbers, or large and small numbered circles. Don't make the numbers too high. Up to 10 will do.

On the base of the box, at the 'top' edge, cut two slits large enough for a coin to pass through.

Cut out coins from card or use plastic counters. Make lots so you don't run out!

The child must push their 'coin' in one slit, and if it lands on a target clear of lines, the child wins the number on the target in 'coins'. There's room for diplomacy here: if the young player is getting to the end of his coins, an extra bonus wouldn't go amiss.

The 'winning' coins are posted back through the second slit, much to the amusement of the child, especially if you are slightly hidden from view!

These are just a few of many creations you can make in box-land! How about:

- making a doll's house as an ongoing project, slowly adding matchbox furniture and pipe-cleaner dolls
- building a complete miniature model village around a village green
- expanding on the puppet theatre by finding new ideas for puppets and writing new scripts

Box-land is a world of fantasy and imagination. Have fun with the children and enjoy the creation process with them. When the box finally gives up its struggle to survive under such heavy play conditions, make something else. After all, you haven't wasted a penny!

Puppets

There are all sorts of puppets you can make from many different bits and pieces from around the house. These puppets can be used with the theatre described in box-land.

Wooden-Spoon Puppet
You will need:
>   a wooden spoon
>   a marker pen
>   a piece of cloth big enough to cover a hand
>   a little yarn for hair
>   glue
>   an elastic band or hair band

Draw a face on the round part of the wooden spoon and cut short lengths of yarn to stick in place for the hair.

Gather the cloth around the base of the spoon (around the 'neck' of the puppet) and secure in place with an elastic band or a 'scrunchie' hair band to make a ruffle around the neck. Hold the handle of the spoon under the cloth to work the puppet.

Straw Celebrities
You will need:

> drinking straws
> pictures of celebrities cut out from magazines or newspapers
> thin card
> adhesive tape
> glue

Stick the celebrity cut-outs on to thin card and cut round carefully. Attach the celebrity puppet to the drinking straw by fixing a piece of adhesive tape to the back of the puppet and around the straw, making sure the top end of the straw is hidden, behind the picture.

Finger Puppets
You will need:

> a marker pen
> small pieces of cloth
> cloth glue or a needle and thread
> short lengths of yarn

Make tubes of cloth to fit over fingers. Stick or sew in place and stick or sew the top edges together. Draw a face on one side. Stick or sew yarn in place for hair. Make all different colours and characters. Small hats can be made using card or paper, or big ears can be cut out of card or cloth, and attached to the puppets.

Glove Puppets
You will need:

> pieces of cloth large enough to go around
>   a hand at least twice
> decoration such as a frill to go
>   round the neck
> sewing thread and a
>   needle
> pieces of felt and
>   glue for features –
>   or a marker pen
> yarn for hair.

Cut two pieces of cloth large enough to fit the puppeteer's hand. Two arms will accommodate the small finger and thumb, and the middle fingers will fit into the head part. This will give the puppet good flexibility.

With the right sides together, sew firmly around all the edges leaving the bottom edge open. Snip the seams up to the stitching line on the curved parts, to stop the cloth from pulling. Take up the hem all around the bottom edge.

Stick small pieces of felt cut out in the shape of features to the face of the puppet and stick lengths of yarn in place for hair. Add a frill around the neck if required.

Glove puppets can be animals as well as people. Add some long, furry ears or a piggy nose to create all sorts of interesting characters. Let your imagination run wild!

Wool Dollies

Wool dollies were very popular toys many years ago. They can be small and used as badges with a safety pin in the back, or larger and played with as regular dolls. You can even make clothes for them!

For a basic doll you will need:
>   a small ball of yarn
>   firm card
>   scissors
>   contrasting yarn to make features
>   a sewing needle.

To make a doll around 6in (15cm) tall, cut one piece of card 6in (15cm) by 4in (10cm) and another piece, 5in (13cm) by 4in (10cm).

When you have made a doll you can see how they are made and adjust these sizes according to how large or small you would like the finished toy to be. Make a whole family or lots of small ones to play with in a classroom scenario.

Take up your small ball of yarn. Position the single strand of yarn so it lies flat along the middle of the larger piece of card with the end held firmly on one short edge. Wrap the yarn around the card from front to back, round and round between twenty and fifty times depending on the thickness of the yarn and what size you want your dolly to be. Try out a few different styles until you get the right one. Don't worry about wasting the yarn. Up to the point where you cut it to make the hair etc. you can simply unravel it and start again.

When you have wound the yarn around the card, cut the strand so that it reaches the top edge and remove the wound yarn from the card, keeping it from tangling. Tie – very tightly – a short length of matching yarn around the top of the loops, about $\frac{1}{2}$ to 1cm down, and snip the ends to form the 'hair'. A little further down, tie a length of yarn round the loops to form the 'neck' and then again to form the waist.

After the waist has been defined, separate the remaining loops in half, to make legs, and tie a short length of yarn very tightly around the bottom of both legs leaving about ½–1cm loops. Then snip through the loops. These frayed edges are the feet of your doll.

Now repeat the winding of yarn around the shorter of the two pieces of card and remove as before. Carefully push this wound yarn through the body part of your dolly to form the arms. Tie a length of yarn close to the ends and snip as before to make the hands. And voila! A wool dolly. To finish off, sew very small backstitches in contrasting yarn or thread to form the features.

A simple smock dress can be made by gently gathering a small piece of cloth either with a running stitch or threading elastic through a hem, and slipping over the doll's head.

A Bedtime Fairy Story to Read Aloud

Fairy stories have always been a favourite bedtime treat. Some of the old-style stories could be frightening and rather harsh in content. This story has been written for today's children with a hint of magic to delight and inspire them.

Ritchie Meets a Giant Spider

Ritchie was hiding in his dad's garden shed. Aunt Lily had come to visit and, although he quite liked her, he hated that red-lipstick kiss she always planted on his cheek. So, he thought if he hid in here for a while, when she found him, she might forget the dreaded kiss!

He heard voices. Oh no, Mum was taking Aunt Lily round the garden. He was sure to be found now. Just as the voices got nearer to the door, something very strange happened. A light flashed somewhere, and Ritchie found himself inside a giant flowerpot. He turned around to see what had happened and came face to face with a fairy! No! It wasn't possible. He rubbed his eyes. He must have fallen asleep and this was a dream.

'No, you're not dreaming,' said the fairy, as if she knew what Ritchie was thinking.

'But . . . but where am I?' Ritchie stuttered.

'You're hiding in one of your dad's flowerpots. You don't want Aunt Lily to catch you, do you?' said the fairy.

'Well, no, but how did YOU know? And how did I get into a flowerpot? I'm far too big!'

'Not at the moment, you're not!' laughed the fairy. 'Ssshh!' she said, suddenly, and they both heard the shed door open.

'Well, he's not in here,' Aunt Lily was saying. 'I wonder where he's got to.'

'Never mind,' said Ritchie's mum. 'Let's go and have a cup of tea. He'll turn up soon.'

The shed door closed and Ritchie and the fairy both let out their breath with a loud 'phew!'.

Then Ritchie asked, 'But how did I get in a flowerpot anyway? And who are you?'

The fairy giggled.

'My name's Lily too and I put a magic spell on you so you could join my world for a while!'

'Great. It means I didn't get caught. But how do we get out of this flowerpot?' It seemed far too difficult to climb up the smooth sides and he couldn't jump that high.

'Yes, you can,' said Lily, reading his thoughts.

'Yes, I can what?' Ritchie asked. He was sure he hadn't actually said anything. He would have to be careful what he thought about in front of Lily.

'Bend your knees a little and pretend you're on a spring!' Lily said. He did, and as he took a little jump off his imaginary spring, he leaped into the air and landed on the top edge of the flowerpot. He looked around, and realised he was still in his dad's garden shed. But he was miniature sized. He was just thinking that this could be fun when a spider crawled along near him. Ritchie fell backwards with shock and tumbled right back into the flowerpot. Lily laughed.

'I thought you wanted to get out!' she said.

'But there's a giant spider up there!' he answered.

'It's just a regular-sized spider – it's you who's the wrong size!' laughed Lily. 'Come on,' she went on, 'be brave. I'll help you.'

Ritchie was cross with himself. Fancy a fairy – a girl fairy at that – not being scared when he was. He'd always thought he was the bravest.

'You can't be brave over everything,' Lily said, reading his mind again. 'You'll soon get used to the "giant spiders". They are quite friendly when you get to know them.'

'Well, if you say so.' Ritchie wasn't very sure but he decided to take Lily's word for it and they both got ready to spring out of the flowerpot.

Whoosh! Lily and Ritchie jumped onto the top edge of the flowerpot. Luckily the spider had crawled away and Ritchie didn't have to face him this time. Lily was jumping from pot to pot and laughing.

'Come on!' she called back to Ritchie. 'Follow me!'

It wasn't as easy as Lily made it look, jumping from pot to pot. The edges were slippery, and more than once Ritchie went tumbling in one. Every time he fell in he got up and quickly jumped out again, just in case there was a giant insect lurking around.

Lily was already at the other end of the bench and she called back to Ritchie, 'Come on – you're very slow!'

'I've never done this before!' he called back to her, concentrating hard on not slipping backwards again. He was going to be black and blue with bruises tomorrow.

'I'm only teasing!' Lily called back. 'Take your time. I'll sit here and watch.' Ritchie wasn't sure he wanted an audience, but he got one anyway and he managed to get right to the end where Lily was without falling over again. She laughed and clapped her hands.

'Well done!' she said. 'Do you want a game of football?'

'Er, I think my football will be far too big for us to push around, let alone play football with,' Ritchie said.

'That's all right. We can use mine. I've got hundreds!' Lily was sitting on the bench next to a bowl of dried peas that Ritchie's dad was going to plant in the garden.

'I lose a few, but your dad doesn't mind. Mostly he blames the mice!' They both reached into the bowl and took a dried pea each, the roundest ones they could find, and dribbled their 'footballs' all around the bench, amongst the flowerpots and packets of seeds. Ritchie stopped playing for a moment and lay down next to a garden trowel. It was bigger than him! Wouldn't everyone be shocked to see him this small!

'Phew! I've had enough of that,' Lily was saying. 'It would be better if it was tidier in here.'

'Maybe we could tidy up a bit?' said Ritchie.

'No, I thought of that, but we can't. Imagine what your dad would say if he thought someone else had been in here.'

'I didn't think of that,' said Ritchie, 'but later, when I'm back to normal, I could tidy up, couldn't I? Then we could play a proper game.' Lily laughed.

'Sure – if you like. Won't your dad be surprised when he finds you tidying up his shed for him! Let's go outside. The sun's shining and we can easily hide from Aunt Lily in the flowers and long grass.'

She squeezed through a gap in the wooden slats of the shed and jumped on to the grass below. Ritchie followed and Lily called to him to bend his knees when he landed. He did, but too much, and went bouncing back up in the air.

'Just a little!' Lily laughed. 'Don't bend them so much.' He got it right the third time and sat on the grass a bit dizzy.

'See those tall, white flowers over there?' Lily said.

'Er, yeah,' Ritchie saw the tall, white flowers she was pointing at. He'd never noticed them before.

'They're called lilies, like me. Come on, we'll be able to see over the tops of all the other flowers in the garden.' They ran over to the lilies.

'Jump!' she said. 'Like you did before.' They both bent their knees and jumped. Whoosh! Lily landed on the lowest petal of a flower. Ritchie, who hadn't been looking where he was going, landed on a shiny leaf, and promptly slid down on to the grass again. Ritchie tutted to himself and tried again. This time he landed on the very edge of a large petal and Lily pulled him on properly before he fell off again.

They looked around at the garden. It was very bright and colourful and seemed like another world when you were fairy sized. Ritchie decided to have a good look at the garden when he was big again.

Suddenly Lily pointed and said, 'Look your mum and aunt, and they're coming this way. Come on, we'll play behind the shed.'

They both jumped down and bounced with big jumps to the private place where Lily always played.

Ritchie found his super-bouncy ball that he had forgotten about. He pushed it round the side of the shed and it rolled out on to the lawn right at Aunt Lily's feet.

'How strange,' Aunt Lily said, as she bent to pick up the ball.

Ritchie and Lily were keeping very quiet behind the shed. They waited for the grown ups to go past and eventually they did.

Ritchie laughed out loud. 'Right at her feet!' he said.

'You know, I think they might be getting worried. You'd better go back now,' Lily said.

'Well, at least I found my ball,' said Ritchie. 'I thought I'd lost that forever.'

'Come and see me tomorrow!' said Lily.

'Yeah, sure,' said Ritchie, 'but I'll clear up the shed before we have any magic spells!'

There was a flash of light and Ritchie heard Lily's voice calling goodbye as if it was getting further and further away. He suddenly found himself back inside the shed and normal sized again. He opened the door and decided to go and brave the red-lipstick kiss. Anyway, he was hungry after all that bouncing about!

Notes

Notes

Notes

Notes

Notes

Notes

Notes

Notes